MATHEMATICAL SCIENCES, TECHNOLOGY, AND ECONOMIC COMPETITIVENESS

EDITED BY JAMES G. GLIMM

Board on Mathematical Sciences

Commission on Physical Sciences,
Mathematics, and Applications

National Research Council

National Academy Press
Washington, D.C. 1991

Support for this project was provided by the Air Force Office of Scientific Research, the Army Research Office, the Department of Energy, the National Science Foundation, the National Security Agency, and the Office of Naval Research.

Library of Congress Catalog Card No. 91-60253
International Standard Book Number 0-309-04483-9

Copies available for sale from
National Academy Press
2101 Constitution Avenue, NW
Washington, DC 20418
S 333
Printed in the United States of America

PREFACE

The fundamental importance of mathematics to the U.S. technology base, to the ongoing development of advanced technology, and, indirectly, to U.S. competitiveness is well known in scientific circles. However, the declining number of U.S. high school students who decide to seek a career in science or engineering is an important indication that many people do not appreciate how central the mathematical sciences have become to our technological enterprise.

The National Research Council's Board on Mathematical Sciences has prepared this report to underscore the importance of supporting mathematics instruction at all levels, from kindergarten through graduate school, to prepare our youth for successful careers in science and engineering. The report is addressed first to the members of the mathematics community, who must play an active role in effecting quite aggressively the technology transfer that stimulates innovation and puts U.S. industry in a competitive position with its trading partners. Corporate decision makers will also benefit from acquainting themselves with the conclusions drawn in this report: mathematics is useful across the entire product cycle, contributing to making better products, improving quality, and shortening the design cycle. Policy makers at the federal and state levels, college and university administrators, high school teachers, and nonscientists as well may also find instructive this report's discussion of how mathematical and quantitative reasoning have penetrated the real world around us.

To trace the impact of mathematics on U.S. technology necessarily involves making choices. The examples in this report are intended to illustrate the widespread use of mathematical reasoning. The board has focused primarily on the use of such reasoning by mathematical scientists themselves, as defined by their professional training, departmental or professional affiliation, or funding sources. Also included in this discussion are examples of the cross-disciplinary impacts of mathematical scientists working with members of other disciplines. A few examples have been drawn from the mathematically oriented portions of related disciplines, such as engineering and computer science.

A report such as this cannot be exhaustive, nor can it be free of repetition as the same ideas are considered from different viewpoints. Powerful mathematical concepts, once thought to be without practical relevance, affect thinking today in many unrelated fields and, more often than not, it is the mathematician who has discovered such connections. Mathematical models established by engineers for fluid flow turn up in transportation studies and in economics; ideas developed in linear algebra are basic to the large input-output models that describe the national economy. Differential equations describe weather forecasting models, semiconductor behavior, and crystallization of substances; even when the equations differ radically, common methods of solution have often been developed and are widely used not only by mathematicians but also by professionals in many other disciplines who could not function without the tools developed by mathematicians.

While considering such examples of the impact of mathematics, the reader should keep in mind that the distinction between direct and indirect support and between short- and long-range connections cannot be drawn clearly. Neither does the board possess a formula that establishes a numerical relationship between increased support for mathematical research and an increase to the gross national product.

Mathematical principles and ideas manifest themselves in several ways: sometimes the connection is obvious and direct; in other cases the influence is more subtle and long-range in nature. Chapter 2, "Key American Industries," illustrates the use of advanced technology in five major U.S. industries—aircraft, semiconductors and computers, petroleum, automobiles, and telecommunications—and examines how their competitive positions over the past decade have been affected by the industries' access to advanced technology. In chapter 3, "The Product Cycle," 11 technologies widely used in modern manufacturing are examined for the impact of mathematics in such applications as economic planning, simulation, quality control, inventory management, marketing, and maintenance and repair. "The Technology Base," chapter 4, describes some of the mathematical technologies that mathematicians employ in their interactions with industrial clients and also emphasizes the importance of technology transfer—the process of incorporating research results in the design of a commercial product or service. It concludes with some strong recommendations for addressing the training of mathematicians for industrial careers. The overall conclusions and recommendations of the report are summarized in chapter 5. Appendix A describes some noteworthy policy studies on advanced technology in recent years, and Appendix B lists the studies by the mathematical community itself since the appearance of the first David report in 1984 (*Renewing U.S. Mathematics: Critical Resource for the Future*, National Academy Press, Washington, D.C., 1984).

Many people, most of them not associated with the Board on Mathematical Sciences, provided information that aided in the preparation of this report. They include S. Andreou, L. Baxter, S. Bisgaard, I. E. Block, H. Cohen, Y. Deng, B. Enquist, R. Ewing, A. Friedman, P. W. Glynn, B. Irwin, E. Johnson, T. Kailath, D. Kleitman, R. Lundegard, L. Mancini, G. McDonald, S. A. Orszag, A. Packer, G.-C. Rota, D. H. Sharp, M. Sobel, A. Tucker, S. Weidman, M. Wheeler, and M. Wright. One of the board members, James G. Glimm, served as editor of this report. Additional editorial assistance was provided by A. Glimm and H. J. Oser.

Phillip A. Griffiths, *Chairman*
Board on Mathematical Sciences

CONTENTS

MATHEMATICAL SCIENCES, TECHNOLOGY, AND ECONOMIC COMPETITIVENESS

EXECUTIVE SUMMARY

The strength of a nation and the well-being of its citizens are determined to a substantial degree by its technological development and its level of economic organization. The starting point of this report is the broad consensus that advanced technology is a vital component of economic competitiveness. Within this framework, this report documents the importance of quantitative reasoning, supported by computational and mathematical models, to all aspects of the complete product cycle and to the economic competitiveness of U.S. industry.

- The quantitative, mathematical and computational approach is enabling, making possible accomplishments that would otherwise not occur. The design of fuel-efficient transonic aircraft is an example, as are the statistical design of experiments in the drug industry, and image reconstruction and enhancement for medical tomography.

- The quantitative approach leads to successive and dramatic improvement in the design and manufacture of new goods and services. The rapid evolution of computer technology, the design of semiconductor devices, and the design of optical lithography used in the manufacture of these devices are examples. Improved oil recovery derives from models of flows in porous media, the importance of which is underscored by potential disruptions to international oil supplies.

- The quantitative approach is essential to achieving, maintaining, and improving product quality. Tough international competition for the best engineering design of very large-scale integrated (VLSI) circuits (off-line quality control) and in the maintenance

1

of quality through process control (on-line quality control) reflects the application of this approach.

- The quantitative approach addresses novel problems and objectives. The automobile engine has been extensively redesigned for better emission control and fuel efficiency on the basis of models of the combustion process. Computer-based just-in-time (JIT) inventory management, computer-based optimized pattern layout, and computer-aided design offer the possibility of a newly competitive posture for a U.S.-based apparel industry.

- This approach is an ongoing and long-term process. To compete successfully in the global marketplace requires a continuous supply of high-value-added products and, therefore, a national emphasis on high technology. There is no serious challenge to the validity or the success of this approach, nor to the requirement for a strong technology base, which this strategy implies.

Manufacturing is the area in which international economic competition is most intense. It plays the dominant role (approximately 60 percent) in world trade. For this reason, the advanced technology and competitiveness of the manufacturing process are important concerns of this report. Service is the larger part of the U.S. economy (70 percent), and it represents a growing portion of the export sector. Efficiency gains will be greatly multiplied if they are realized in this sector as well. Thus this report also discusses the role of technology and quantitative thinking in the service sector. Technology and quantitative thinking contribute to the competitiveness of all economic sectors.

In addition to the creation of technology, its transfer into new goods and services is of central importance. In view of the continuous web of ideas that make up the intellectual life of our nation, it seems most practical to create technology and to promote its transfer broadly for all segments of the economy, even though the concerns of this report relate most directly to support for the manufacturing sector.

Technology transfer will have occurred when a new idea, a new method, or a new process has been successfully incorporated into a product or service. Active cooperation among the research group, the design engineers, and the manufacturing team presents the ideal climate for rapid technology transfer. The Board on Mathematical Sciences views advanced technology and its transfer as essential for the economic viability and leadership of our nation, and deems it the responsiblity of all participants, users and producers of the technology base, to foster that transfer actively.

Findings

- **The mathematical sciences are vital to economic competitiveness. They are a critical, generic, enabling technology.**

This principal finding is elaborated further by these observations:

- Applications of the mathematical sciences arise in all aspects of the product cycle and across the technology base.

- Applications also arise from highly diverse areas of the mathematical sciences; they depend on the vitality of research in the mathematical sciences and draw on this research as a technology base.

- Computation and modeling recur as central themes. They are a primary route for technology transfer from the mathematical sciences.

- Technology transfer, from the research to the industrial sector, is of critical importance for the enhancement of economic competitiveness.

- In the mathematical sciences (as elsewhere), technology transfer occurs seriously below its potential. The transfer of technology will be accomplished best if the creators of technology assume the primary responsibility for its transfer. Also helpful is an atmosphere of cooperation among the industrial, governmental, and academic sectors, an atmosphere in which the central importance of technology transfer is clearly understood by the participants in the process.

- Technology transfer, computational and mathematical modeling, and education have an importance to economic competitiveness that is very large relative to the recognition given to these activities by the academic mathematical sciences community.

- Manpower and technical training are also crucial for economic competitiveness. The mathematical sciences community has a significant responsibility in this area.

The ability of the mathematical sciences community to deliver short-term results with any degree of consistency depends crucially on healthy support for its long-term development. Engineering and manufacturing research and design depend heavily on computational and mathematical modeling. The mathematical sciences community has the primary responsibility for the collegiate mathematics education of engineers and scientists and has taken a leadership role in efforts to revitalize mathematics education at all levels. These three issues, long-term health and renewal of the mathematical sciences community, computation and mathematical modeling, and education and manpower training, have been considered in high-level policy studies (see Appendix B for references). The recommendations in this report build on and supplement these studies, and the board specifically endorses the recommendations in the earlier reports.

Recommendations

This report makes two primary recommendations:

- **The board recommends that the mathematical sciences community significantly increase its role in the transfer of mathematical sciences technology.**

- **The board calls on the mathematical sciences community to put far greater emphasis on and give greater career recognition to activities connected with computational and mathematical modeling, technology transfer, and education.**

To ensure that technology transfer occurs, mathematical scientists, engineers, manufacturers, and business leaders must accept the task to be accomplished and plan for the result.

Computational and mathematical modeling, technology transfer, and education have a critical and direct connection to economic competitiveness, a connection that should be reflected in the recognition given these activities by the mathematical sciences community. Specific actions, endorsed by this report, for carrying out its two primary recommendations include the following:

- Federal and state agencies should ensure that investments in research to improve productivity include the necessary involvement and support of the mathematical sciences.

- Programs in industrial mathematics, jointly supported by industry and government, should be established in our colleges and universities and should include grants for small science and for individual investigators.

The economic competitiveness of the United States can be substantially improved by increased involvement of the mathematical sciences community. Numerous agencies currently sponsor programs that have successfully encouraged interaction between academic and government laboratory researchers. This report proposes a similar effort to stimulate increased interaction between universities and industry.

Federally funded science and technology centers already have a mandate for technology transfer. However, many industrial problems in mathematics are of moderate size, appropriate to small science and individual investigators. A formal program in industrial mathematics should therefore take advantage of the contributions that small science and individual investigators can make.

- The board urges that strong and meaningful consideration for hiring, retention, promotion, and tenure be given for achievements in research and education supporting industrial mathematics. The emphasis given to computational mathematics, modeling, and applications should be in balance with that accorded to other areas of mathematics.

- The board calls on university administrators to encourage adoption by their mathematical sciences units of criteria and procedures that promote strengthening of the ties between universities and industry.

Our national requirements for the creation of new mathematical sciences technology, as well as for effective access to this technology, call for a balance between theory and applications.

- The board recommends that industry, government, and university cooperative research and education programs be encouraged and funded.

Cooperation among industry, government, and universities benefits all three. Such cooperation can take many forms, some of which, from the simple consultant relationship to the formation of industrial consortia, are mentioned in this report. Often such cooperation leads to employment for students, after graduation, by the industrial firm. At this point, an important step in completing technology transfer to the industrial sector has taken place.

- The board recommends development of course materials to support the teaching of modeling and of industrial applications of mathematics.

The purpose of this course material would be to narrow the gap between academic mathematics and the industrial uses of mathematics, i.e, problem solving and modeling. The course material should broaden the students' intellectual horizons as well as their technical training. It should increase their potential usefulness in an industrial organization and should increase their ability, as future teachers of mathematics to engineers, to motivate the use of mathematics in an industrial context.

- The board urges the mathematical sciences professional societies to promote intellectual activity in problem solving and modeling to strengthen the industrial use of mathematics.

Technology transfer can occur only with the full support of the people who are actively engaged in the process. The board proposes that the mathematical professional societies include technology transfer within their mission and encourage, through workshops, minisymposia, and plenary lectures, more interaction among mathematicians in industry, universities, and government laboratories. Special conferences on theoretical areas of mathematics could include the industrial perspective as well. Mathematicians in industry should be encouraged to serve in larger numbers on the editorial boards of professional journals. Much of this framework is in place already, but the evident need to improve on the rate and calibre of technology transfer implies that increased attention to these issues is imperative.

Conclusions

Our industrial environment is undergoing rapid change. The mathematical sciences community can play a significant role in promoting this change in the United States by becoming an active partner in this process.

From engineering design and research to management and organizational structures to the control of smart machines and robots, the computer is leading a revolution that vitally affects the competitiveness of industry and of our entire society. The mathematical sciences are at the basis of many of those changes, and they provide a crucial technology in effecting this revolution. The continuing increase in the range of human and technological activities that can be described in mathematical terms is part of this revolution. Mathematics acts, and achieves its value, through its ability to organize and structure knowledge. The role of the mathematical sciences as a technology is not recognized, nor is the full importance of its role as a force for technological change and industrial competitiveness. This central fact is the basis for this report.

1 INTRODUCTION

The strength of a nation and the well-being of its citizens are determined to a substantial degree by its technological development and its level of economic organization. These determinants of national position are of serious concern precisely because they are now under challenge. High-level reviews of U.S. advanced technology are in agreement with this point of view: consider the 12 emerging technologies identified by the Department of Commerce, the grand challenges associated with the Federal High Performance Computing Program, the 20 critical technologies identified by the departments of Defense and Energy, and the report by the Technology Policy Task Force of the Committee on Science, Space and Technology of the U.S. House of Representatives (Appendix A). Running through these studies and the accompanying public discussion is a concern for the future viability of the long-held technological leadership of the United States.

A range of opinions exists concerning the importance of factors shaping a country's ability to be economically competitive. Such discussions are outside the scope of this report, which takes as its starting point the broad consensus that advanced technology is a vital component of economic competitiveness. The report documents the importance of quantitative reasoning, supported by computational and mathematical models, to all aspects of the complete product cycle and to economic competitiveness. In addition, it identifies some prominent opportunities for enhancing U.S. competitiveness in the future.

Dividing the U.S. economy into sectors provides useful insight. Service makes up approximately 70 percent, manufacturing 20 percent, and construction, mining, and agriculture the remaining 10 percent (*Economic Report of the President*, 1989 [1]). From the perspective of world trade, the division of the U.S. economy is very different. The share of manufacturing is 57 percent, mining and agriculture are each about 10 percent, transportation and travel are each about 6 percent, and the balance is 11 percent (Passel, 1990 [2]). Manufacturing, the area in which international economic competition is most intense, plays a dominant role in export and import, and thus is given major emphasis in this report. Also discussed is the role of technology and quantitative thinking in the service sector, because the benefits of increases in productivity will be greatly multiplied if they are realized in this sector as well. Most sectors of our economy (service, agriculture, government, national security and defense, and manufacturing) have already benefited greatly from the introduction of U.S. advanced technology.

Major U.S. industries with a trade deficit (automobiles, oil, consumer electronics), those with a trade surplus (aircraft manufacture, chemicals), and those that are emerging or have a strategic importance for the future (biotechnology, computers) depend on advanced technology and quantitative reasoning, not only for research and development, but also through all stages of the product cycle, including especially the manufacturing process itself.

Both advanced technology and economic analysis are implemented in quantitative terms. From the strategic planning for large organizations, to the design of novel or superior products, to the assessment of risk and safety factors and the engineering of reliable products, quantitative thinking has been critical to success. Quantitative thinking typically implies the formulation and modeling of a problem in mathematical terms and the simulation and solution of the model equations, often using computational methods. It necessarily requires validation and parameter adjustment through laboratory and field data. It is often interdisciplinary in nature.

Examples of clear quantitative and mathematical successes that have an impact on advanced technology and economic competitiveness are widespread. This fact can be verified by examining the complete product cycle, from strategic planning to research, engineering design, manufacturing efficiency, process control, quality improvement, marketing, inventory, transportation, distribution, and product maintenance. There are similar examples within the technology base, outside of specific product cycles, such as the advanced computational methods that serve weather forecasting needs. The simulation of physical phenomena, optimization, scheduling methods, nonlinear partial differential equations, and statistical and mathematical models are ideas that arise both in the support of the technology base and in specific economic and technological endeavors. The report will show that

- The quantitative, mathematical, and computational approach is enabling, making possible accomplishments that would otherwise not occur. The design of fuel-efficient transonic aircraft is an example.

- This approach allows successive and dramatic improvement. The rapid evolution of computer technology is an example.

- This approach is essential to achieving, maintaining, and improving product quality. An example is the maintenance of quality through process control.

- This approach addresses novel problems and objectives. The redesign of the automotive engine to emphasize emission control and fuel efficiency is an example.

- This approach is an ongoing and long-term process. To compete successfully in the global marketplace requires a continuous supply of high-value-added products. Our nation must, therefore, emphasize high technology, which is intensively quantitative, from planning to design to production. There is no serious challenge to the validity or the success of this approach, nor to the requirement for a strong technology base, which this strategy implies.

The many changes in worldwide political structures, such as the coming economic unification of western Europe, the growing economic power of the nations of the Pacific rim, and the changing trade patterns and decrease in military tensions in central Europe, have led to a vision of a new world order. We can expect increasing economic competition among nations, and that this competition will be increasingly important. These changes only serve to emphasize the invariance of the central fact that leadership in advanced technology and the maintenance of a strong technology base are essential to the continued strength and competitive position of our nation. One competitive advantage of the

United States is its world leadership in the theory and application of computing. The importance of this fact to economic competitiveness is illustrated throughout this report. Further advantages of the United States are its position in basic research and its strong university system. The mathematical sciences are an especially strong component of U.S. science. These strengths must be preserved, and they must be brought to bear on problems of competitiveness, if this country is to maintain its position into the next century.

The central conclusion of this report is that the mathematical sciences are vital to economic competitiveness and that they are a critical, generic, and enabling technology. This conclusion is examined from three points of view. In chapter 2, key industries are examined from the point of view of their competitive positions, their dependence on advanced technology, and the role that the mathematical sciences have played in support of advanced technology. The industries selected are not exceptional, and the same points could have been made through the examination of a number of different industries. Chapter 3 considers key economic functions and activities; 11 steps in the product cycle are examined in some detail for their mathematical components. These steps cover the entire product cycle, from economic planning for new products to maintenance and repair of the manufactured goods. Case studies illustrate the mathematical contributions found in the entire product cycle. In chapter 4 the mathematical sciences technology base for economic competitiveness is considered, and the role of mathematics in technology transfer and education is discussed.

The uses of mathematics described in this report generally involved the creation of new mathematics, a proof of principle, or an initial reduction of a mathematical result to practice. All three of these activities are legitimate mathematical research issues. In almost every case, these applications raise new mathematical issues, which, the board believes, is the reason they were carried out by mathematicians, rather than by scientists or engineers from other fields.

Industrial mathematics is defined in this report as applicable mathematics that is used in an industrial context. Its value to a final product or service varies from one context to another but in general can be categorized as helpful, enabling, or critical. The board does not attempt to determine which of the examples cited in this report fall into each of these three categories.

This report discusses representative selections of the many mathematical areas that have been used to develop advanced technology and and thus have contributed to improving U.S. economic competitiveness. This discussion cannot be complete for a simple reason: most of mathematics would then be included, either directly or indirectly.

The major findings and recommendations of this report are summarized in chapter 5. The report concludes with a list of references and two appendices, one with a list of pertinent governmental, industrial and academic policy studies, the other with studies conducted by the mathematical sciences community over the past 8 years.

2 KEY AMERICAN INDUSTRIES

In this chapter's review of the positions of five American industries, the following questions are addressed: What is their competitive position? To what extent do they utilize advanced technology? What use do they make of quantitative reasoning and computational and mathematical modeling?

A thorough study of the correlation between competitiveness and technology would require further analysis, which is beyond the scope of this report. The industries surveyed here all depend very strongly on technology. With the partial exception of the automotive industry, the mathematical sciences have a long and deep history of involvement with the technological bases of these industries. The automotive industry and the petroleum industry are the largest contributors to the U.S. trade deficit. The U.S. petroleum industry is resource-limited and is strongly competitive in its international operations. Telecommunications is the only service industry analyzed in this chapter. It is noteworthy among service industries for its continually improved products at decreasing costs, achieved through the successful use of technology. This success of telecommunications is not unique within the service sector. Other service industries that have achieved success through organizational innovation and technology include the airline and financial services industries.

The United States is part of a global economy. In order to purchase goods and services on the global market, we must also sell them. We sell a wide range of products, from lumber to jet airliners. Lumber is an example of a "low-tech" industry. Many countries have trees to sell on the world market. The prices that can be charged for them are constrained by this competition, and wages in the U.S. lumber industry are not high by U.S. standards. Aircraft is an example of a "high-tech" industry. Wages tend to be higher in the aircraft industry and other high-tech industries than in lumber and other low-tech industries. Much of our country's future economic well-being, then, depends on our ability to establish and maintain competitive positions in industries in which the value added by our labor is high.

The extent of the problem of competitiveness for U.S. industry can be indicated by the following statistics [3].

In 1989 the service sector generated a $20 billion trade surplus while manufacturing trade produced a $115 billion trade deficit. Petroleum imports produced a $50 billion trade deficit, while agriculture produced a moderate surplus. Current accounts were settled in part through the $72 billion worth of companies and real estate that were purchased by foreign investors in the same year. To paraphrase the discussion of *Made in America* [4], it will not be possible to close the trade gap through growth in the service sector. On the other hand, Quinn [5] argues that in the service sector high-technology capital investment has been rising rapidly since the mid-1960s. In fact, the service sector depends on manufacturing for its vitality, and cannot be expected to remain healthy while manufacturing continues to lose ground. Figures 2.1–2.4 show a consistent loss of U.S. market share for U.S. manufacturing across many industries over the last decade.

Several conclusions can be drawn from the analysis in this chapter. The historic record of economic success for the United States cannot be taken for granted in the future. Technology is an important aspect of economic success. The mathematical sciences are nearly always an integral part of that technology, both on the basis of computational simulation[1] and on the basis of quantitative reasoning and modeling. Technology applies to all phases of the product cycle and is not simply a research and development activity. It is most effective when the interrelations among these phases are considered, such as the relations among

---

[1] *Simulation* includes mathematical modeling and heuristic principles in order to represent on a computer real-world processes and systems (e.g., rush-hour traffic in a metropolitan area, the real-time operations of a large telephone network, or the flow of air around an aircraft). Computational and numerical analysis play a role in simulation. The distinction between *simulation* and *computation*, as defined here, is illustrated by the fact that a correct simulation must agree with the real-world process being simulated, whereas a correct computation must agree only with the mathematical model or equation being solved.

product design, cost, and quality. In fact, simultaneous attention to production efficiency, production quality, and consumer requirements seems to be necessary for competitive success in a manufacturing industry.

The MIT Commission on Industrial Productivity, in its study [4], cites six contributing factors present in many of the areas where the U.S. competitive position has been weakened.

- Outdated strategies

- Short time horizons

- Technological weaknesses in development and production

- Neglect of human resources

- Failure of cooperation

- Government and industry at cross-purposes

Several of these factors are discussed in this report; technological weakness is the central concern. Technical training and education are a major means of maximizing human resources. The mathematical sciences community is making a substantial effort to improve mathematics education and training. Problems with technology transfer are a major aspect of the failure of cooperation. Short time horizons result in a systematic undervaluation of research and development. There is a possible technical basis for this undervaluation, in the neglect of the option value in decision making, as is discussed in §3.1. Research and development are important largely because of their option value. One aspect of outdated strategies is the promotion of standardized products for mass markets. As markets become more fragmented to serve individualized customer tastes and needs, flexible manufacturing and inventory control become important technical issues, which are being addressed through mathematical modeling.

2.1 Aircraft

Commercial aircraft manufacture enjoys a strong positive balance of payments. This is true despite the fact that U.S. dominance of the

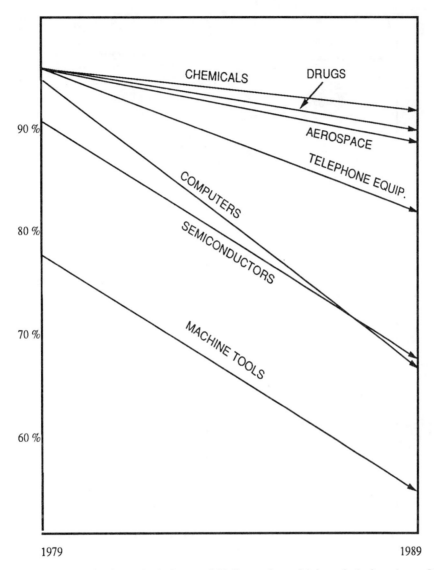

FIGURE 2.1 U.S. factories' share of U.S. market: high-tech industries. Over the past decade, the loss by U.S. factories of domestic market share in high-technology industries averaged 0.9 percentage points per year on a dollar weighted basis. The total market loss was $45 billion from a total market of $518 billion. Total U.S. manufacturing employment in these industries decreased from 1.66 million to 1.39 million, or 1.7 percentage points per year. Adapted, by permission, from [3]. Copyright ©1990 by the Time Magazine Co.

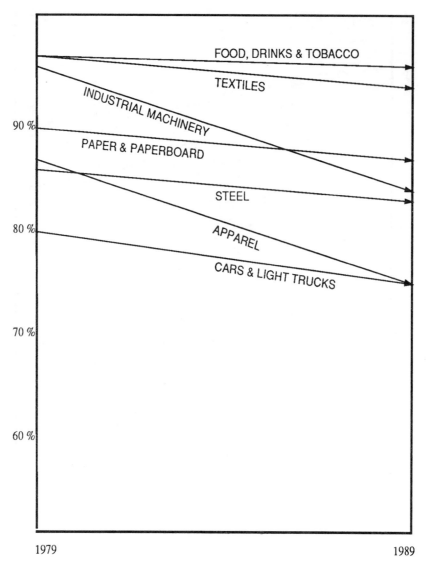

1979   1989

FIGURE 2.2 U.S. factories' share of U.S. market: other industries I. U.S. factories in major industries with a combined annual market value of $728 billion and manufacturing employment of 3.82 million have lost domestic market share at an average rate of 0.4 percentage points per year over the past decade. The total market loss was $28.5 billion. Over the past decade, the total U.S. manufacturing employment in these industries decreased from 4.23 million to 3.41 million, or 2.1 percentage points per year. Adapted, by permission, from [3]. Copyright ©1990 by the Time Magazine Co.

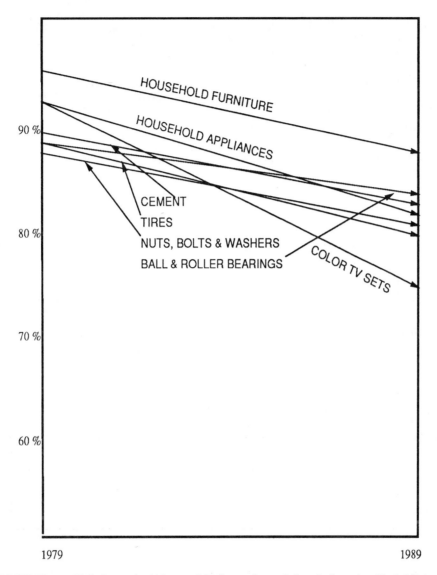

FIGURE 2.3 U.S. factories' share of U.S. market: Other industries II. Additional major industries with a combined market value of $66 billion annually and manufacturing employment of 0.58 million show a similar pattern of decrease in domestic market share and total employment. Adapted, by permission, from [3]. Copyright ©1990 by the Time Magazine Co.

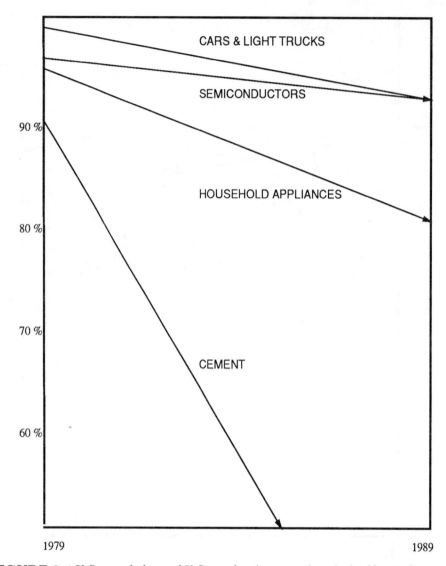

FIGURE 2.4 U.S-owned share of U.S. production capacity. A significant decrease in the U.S.-owned share of U.S. production capacity occurred in a number of industries over the past decade. Adapted, by permission, from [3]. Copyright ©1990 by the Time Magazine Co.

marketplace is now challenged by Airbus, a heavily subsidized competitor from Europe. In the United States, a high degree of cooperation in this area exists among industry, government, and academia. NASA has sponsored studies of aircraft design, while military procurement has aided the development of commercial manufacturing facilities. However, owing to the divergence of military and commercial aircraft technologies, the commercial aircraft industry may receive less benefit from these sources in the future. For these reasons, the continued competitive position of the domestic aircraft manufacturing industry cannot be taken for granted.

The importance of the mathematical sciences to the competitive position of the aircraft industry is developed in §3.2 and again in §3.11. A brief summary of those sections follows. In aircraft design, fuel efficiency and speed are key factors that influence sales. The design of aircraft is based to a very large extent on computation, which is necessary to solve equations that describe the flow field around the wing and the complete airframe. Numerical analysis is a critical technology in the development of the computer codes needed for the design work. Included here is the algorithm development for fluid flow, grid generation, and structural analysis. Structural analysis, flutter, and vibration are studied by finite element methods. Stability of control elements has been analyzed by control theory. Engineering design and manufacturing depend on computer-aided design (CAD) and computer-aided manufacturing (CAM), which depend on mathematical tools for their theoretical bases. Computational fluid dynamics (CFD) helps in the design of new aircraft and defines the most important wind tunnel tests. CFD favorably affects the time available for the aeronautical engineers when a particular airplane configuration must be "frozen" in order to begin with the design of the manufacturing process. Repair protocols used in aircraft maintenance facilities have been strongly influenced by operational analysis.

2.2   Semiconductors and Computers

The transistor and the computer are American inventions. Until the 1980s, the U.S. industry was dominant worldwide. In the last decade, Japanese corporations have dominated the semiconductor industry, with a 50 percent market share, and a much higher share for memory chips. These companies have established an increasingly competitive position in computers. Various explanations have been advanced for the loss of the U.S. competitive position, including dumping and restrictive trade practices by Japan, fragmentation of the U.S. semiconductor industry into a multitude of start-up firms, and the differences in interest rates and planning time horizons, both favoring Japanese companies. However, these explanations are peripheral in comparison to the absolute dominance of Japanese firms in manufacturing. Their superiority is evident in speed, quality, and especially in the incremental introduction of new technology. The computer industry is at the heart of most high-technology developments, and so its strategic value is enormous, both in terms of projected future markets and in its influence on the rest of the economy. For this reason, a number of studies have been directed to the question of how to support this industry and to prevent further erosion of its competitive position. (See *A Strategic Industry at Risk* [6], cited in Appendix A.9.)

Computation and mathematical modeling are essential tools for the design of various computer components. The importance of these methods is likely to increase as the technology advances and as forces of economic competitiveness require shorter development times from the conception of a technology to its introduction in the marketplace. The design and fabrication of today's chip necessitate many computational tools. To predict the electrical characteristics of semiconductor devices, designers have to solve differential equations that govern the flow of the holes and the electrons. The rapid change of electrical properties within these devices (at gate edges) leads to stiff differential equations, for which numerical methods have been developed. The layout of gates and devices on a chip is a complex problem, which has been addressed by discrete optimization methods and by simulated annealing. Computation and modeling are used in preparing the masks that are used to fabricate the chips. The testing of the manufactured chip to ensure that its millions of parts function as designed poses a difficult computational problem, for which several combinatorial and statistical methods have been developed. And finally, the structural properties of the packaging have to be simulated to predict heat-induced stresses.

The design of magnetic discs is equally demanding of computational simulation tools. The magnetic field generated, the micro-magnetic forces within the disc head, the air flow around the head, and the mechanical properties of the disc head subassembly are all important for the design and development of modern discs. Computational methods are indispensable to the engineer who is engaged in disc design, replacing the expensive and time-consuming construction of physical prototypes. Mathematics has played an important role in the development of the codes used to store the information on magnetic discs. Symbolic dynamics provided a methodology for encoding information with maximal efficiency.

Computation and mathematical modeling are important aspects of the technical support for sales, through modeling of customers' technical problems. Software development and methods of numerical computation are areas of competitive strength for the United States. The computer industry maintains a substantial in-house effort in the mathematical sciences and has strong academic ties to support the development of numerical methods.

2.3   Petroleum

The petroleum industry originated and first reached prominence in the United States. Today, although the U.S. industry is highly competitive in international exploration and production, its domestic operations are limited by the availability of natural resources. Most of the remaining domestic reserves are located in high-cost, marginal, or economically depleted fields. As a consequence, the industry is one of the two largest contributors to the U.S. balance of payments deficit. The deficit associated with imported petroleum in 1989 was $50 billion [3]. Moreover, the trade deficit owing to the amount of imported petroleum is likely to increase and has the potential to increase at a significant rate, as one can see from the rate of decline of U.S. oil production in the years preceding the Alaskan North Slope discoveries. A structural problem of this industry is the need to prevent or delay the abandonment of marginal fields, while awaiting the development of cost-effective enhanced oil recovery methods or some future increase in petroleum prices that would justify production of the residual oil. It is commonly estimated that after conventional production, about two-thirds of the original oil remains in place. Therefore the marginal or economically depleted fields are important as a potential future resource. In addition to the major producers, there are many independent operators. The technical level of the independents varies, but it is fair to say that it is totally impossible for them to match the technical expertise of the major producers. Technology support and transfer therefore become very important issues.

Two critical technologies that address the problems of the domestic petroleum industry are the characterization of reservoir geology and the prediction of fluid flow patterns through this geology. Characterization is needed to identify classes of reservoirs most at risk of abandonment that also have the largest potential for future production. It is also needed as a preliminary step in the prediction of fluid flow patterns and in the design of enhanced oil recovery projects. The fluid flow patterns are needed to guide future development, for example, to set the location of additional wells.

In order to model the flow of oil through porous media, it is important to have a true representation of the geological strata and their properties that characterize the behavior of the flow. Figure 2.5 represents a model geology used to test the validity of the method. Figure 2.6 shows the structure that was derived from measurements of the reflected signals at many different recording stations. Such "synthetic" models are important for estimating the accuracy of the method chosen for the signal analysis.

Reservoir characterization depends on geostatistics, random fields, signal processing, Fourier analysis, and the solution of the wave and elasticity equations for the interpretation of seismic signals. It depends on the solution of an inverse problem known as history matching to reconstruct reservoir geology from oil production records and requires sophisticated modeling of well-logging tools. Reservoir characterization makes extensive use of computations. Fluid flow patterns in reservoirs are the central concern in petroleum reservoir engineering. They are studied computationally and depend on finite element, finite difference, and adaptive mesh refinement methods; fast Fourier transforms; free boundary problems; and nonlinear conservation laws. In the future, parallel computing will play a large role. Mathematical scientists have been involved in most or all phases of these studies (see Figure 2.7).

Many other technologies dependent on the mathematical sciences have been and are being used in the petroleum industry. Scheduling theories and mathematical programming are used to assign destinations

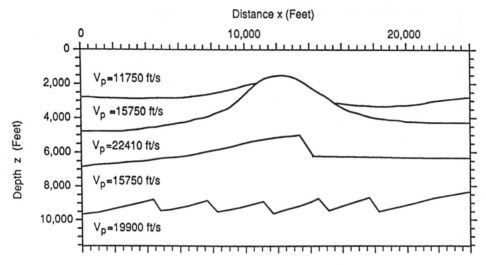

FIGURE 2.5 Marathon model geology for seismic simulation study. Velocity of sound is assumed to be constant in layers separated by curved surfaces. Courtesy of Dong *et al.* [7], Figure 4.

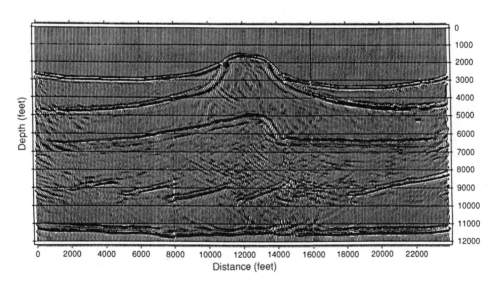

FIGURE 2.6 Reconstruction of geology from seismic inversion, using simulated seismic signals and the model geology shown in Figure 2.5. Courtesy of Dong *et al.* [7], Figure 8.

FIGURE 2.7 Flow pattern in a small portion of an idealized reservoir, with a well for production of petroleum at the upper right corner and a well for the injection of a displacing fluid (e.g., water) at the lower left corner. Shown here is the position of an interface between the two fluids, at four distinct times in the displacement process. The reservoir is heterogeneous, which causes fluid instabilities in the form of fingers. The fingers lead to bypassing of oil and thus reduce total oil recovery. Courtesy of F. Pereira, State University of New York at Stony Brook.

and cargoes to oil tankers. Refinery design and control depend on differential equations and control theory. The cleanup of oil spills can be monitored using fluid flow computations. Novel technologies, such as the use of microbes to degrade hydrocarbons in situ, are understood by computational modeling, before extensive and time-consuming field tests are initiated. Modeling of geological basins depends on computational and mathematical models and is important in the selection of potential sites for exploratory drilling.

2.4 Automobiles

The mass production and assembly line methods on which the automobile industry depends were first invented and developed in the United States. Nonetheless, the industry has been in decline in this country for three decades. The U.S. automobile industry moved from a position of world dominance and a strong export surplus in the 1950s to a weak competitive position in the 1980s. This industry is one of the two largest contributors to our present trade deficit, with a 1987 negative trade balance of nearly $60 billion (see [4]). Several factors have been advanced as critical in the decline of this industry. Various commentators have blamed labor, management, or government, or the hostile relations among these sectors. Changes in consumer taste have occurred more rapidly than changes in the industry's product offerings. The primary technical weaknesses concern quality, cost, reliability, and the time required to initiate a new model or design. Automation has been less successful in the United States than in Japan, and important innovations, for example, just-in-time (JIT) inventory control, were first introduced abroad. Recent developments have moderated these negative trends. The quality of U.S. automobiles is now getting closer to that of Japanese cars and is ahead of the European imports.[2]   The last year has seen a 2.6 percent increase in market

---

[2] In its annual ratings of automobiles, *Consumer Reports* uses a five-level scale, ranging from much-better-than-average to much-worse-than-average. An analysis of one- and two-year-old domestic and imported automobiles for which data were available in 1988, 1989, and 1990 shows an average net improvement of one-fifth of a rating step for domestic cars, while the imports slipped by one-third of a step on average. This measure differs from the rating used by J.D. Powers Associates, which is based on surveys of customer satisfaction during the first three months of ownership (see [8]), according to which U.S. automobiles are nearly equal in quality to that of Japanese cars.

share for U.S.-manufactured automobiles, representing a shift from imports to U.S.-built Japanese-brand automobiles. Competition for market share remains intense and is shifting to design questions. Here the competitive advantage of the Japanese companies lies in the speed of their design cycle, which at four years is reported to be well below the U.S. design time. Japan's market share is strongest among younger owners and so has a built-in growth advantage.

Design, engineering, and manufacturing have changed enormously under the influence of the computer. In almost all cases, the computer requires mathematical theories for its successful employment. Starting from an artist's rendering, detailed shape functions are generated by computer-aided design. This construction is based on the theory of splines, which is a polynomial interpolation method whose fundamental theory and applications were developed by mathematical scientists. Shapes are transformed into structural elements through computer-aided engineering (CAE). Here, a complete finite element model of the structure is developed and optimized to produce lighter weight, control vibrations, and assure strength (see Figure 2.8). Many components have their own detailed models. The combustion process in the engine has been modeled computationally to achieve better fuel efficiency and emission control. Computer-aided manufacturing involves the construction of dies and stamps for metal formation, the computer control of lathes and machining equipment, and control of automation for the manufacturing process. It also involves scheduling and routing of work in progress from one station to another and to the design of the factory floor layout. Mathematical methods have served as an input to important aspects of the CAD/CAE/CAM process.

Mathematical ideas and tools are used to solve a broad spectrum of automotive industry problems. Strategic economic planning has been improved to include the option value of decision choices. Since the future value of research is almost exclusively an option value (i.e., it allows but does not require future decisions to be made or options to be exercised), the need for these methods in the evaluation of research is evident. Operations research was used to solve market strategy problems, such as the fleet mix problem, to achieve the best mix of different vehicles to be produced that met given miles/gallon requirements.

The importance of advanced technology is captured in the following

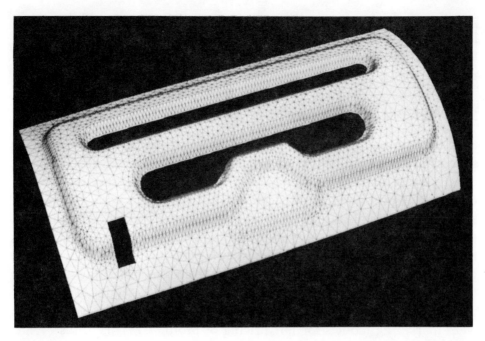

FIGURE 2.8 The complex functional geometry of this automobile inner panel was designed and represented using new feature-based surface design methods developed at the General Motors Research Laboratories. The triangular mesh shown on the surface was computed automatically by relying on the same feature information used to design the part. Thus the feature-based surface representation can serve as a link between the design and automated field emission microscopy analysis of the part. Figure courtesy of General Motors Research Laboratories.

question and its answer. Which country will be a strong competitor in the world auto market? The one that best succeeds in shortening the design process, improving manufacturing, and meeting customers' needs (see [9]).

2.5   Telecommunications

Telecommunications is a noteworthy example of an economically successful service industry. Major accomplishments have been to pioneer new technologies, lower unit costs, and expand service offerings consistently over a period of decades. Major research achievements basic to the growth of this industry include the invention of the transistor, developmental work in computers and operating systems, and work on fiber optics. The industry has been very successful in the design of semiconductor devices, which are required for telephone switching networks. Queuing theory, information theory, and coding theory for signal compression were developed within the telecommunications industry, as were marketing models for fair pricing of products. This industry has been a leader in the development and use of statistical quality control methods. The telecommunications industry moved rapidly to exploit a major breakthrough in the design of interior point methods for linear programming, applying them to the design of optimal switching networks. These methods are broadly applicable to a wide range of problems and have been adopted, e.g., by the airline industry, for the solution of scheduling problems. This industry is also a leader in the development of statistical and mathematical models of speech. It has been a leader in the early development of mathematical models of the physiology of the human ear. The mathematical sciences have been strongly represented in the telecommunications industry, which maintains close relations with academic mathematical scientists who have also investigated many of the above topics.

The 1980s saw the implementation of the first telephone network management scheme, which looks at the entire nationwide network as one sharable resource and replaces the previous hierarchical schemes, which divided the country into regions and imposed restrictions on sharing. The concepts and design for this nonhierarchical network are rooted in mathematics (queues, stochastic networks, teletraffic, and mathematical programming) and were developed at AT&T Bell Labo-

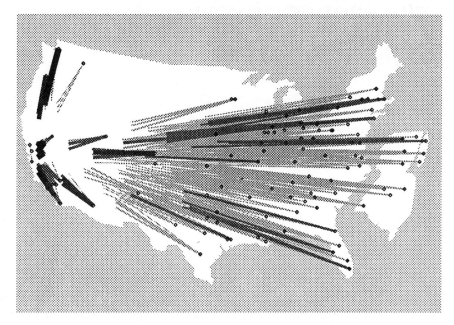

FIGURE 2.9 This figure shows the traffic calling pattern in the AT&T network 30 minutes after the 1989 California earthquake. The shaded lines indicate increases in call volumes above normal. The network is designed and maintained using a linear programming formulation for normal traffic patterns. Following the earthquake, outbound traffic was given priority through dynamic network management controls, and extra capacity was allocated for outbound traffic by an adaptive routing algorithm. Figure courtesy of AT&T.

ratories over the past decade.

Another significant innovation, real-time state-dependent routing, is currently being implemented. Under this scheme, the state of congestion existing at the time of an individual call is used to determine the call's route. The scheme relies on new technology and new conceptual understanding of network behavior, which in turn is derived from mathematics and simulations (see Figure 2.9).

3 THE PRODUCT CYCLE

The mathematical sciences have played key roles in virtually every aspect of the product cycle, from strategic economic planning to maintenance, repair, and (in the case of hazardous waste) disposal. Inventory, schedule, and transport route planning are all based on mathematical theories. Engineering design is based on the solution of differential equations, often by computational means. Markets are studied by examining statistical samples, allowing optimal choices of product mix to be determined. Optimal strategies are determined by operations research methods. Complex systems are described in terms of probability models. These same methods, including methods of statistical quality control, apply to the manufacturing process as well. This chapter draws on case studies to consider specific approaches, based on the mathematical sciences, to specific economic functions in specific industries.

3.1 Economic Planning

Decision makers involved in financial analysis generally rely on conventional capital budgeting techniques to quantify the dollar value of an investment. These techniques consist of traditional discounted cash flow (DCF) calculations. DCF methods provide a good conceptual framework for evaluating several types of investments. But in many cases, the assumptions required by DCF methods prohibit evaluation of important investment characteristics. For example, future opportunities created by today's investments are often treated as intangibles. Consequently, investments to develop new manufacturing technologies, to achieve differentiation through quality, or to establish operating flexibility may appear too risky, and DCF calculations may indicate that they have negative present values. As a result, investment opportunities in those areas are systematically undervalued, with detrimental consequences for future competitiveness.

To overcome this capital budgeting shortcoming, finance theory has recently provided some very powerful extensions to the traditional methodology. Those extensions are based on what is known as option pricing theory (OPT), or contingent claim analysis. The seminal contributions to OPT were made at MIT in the late 1960s and early 1970s. OPT had a direct and significant impact in practice through its applications in financial markets (pricing of traded "call" and "put" options). Following that success, the possibility of extending OPT to real capital investment decisions was soon realized. As a result, a significant volume of research has been carried out on this topic. By now, it has been well established that option-like characteristics permeate virtually every aspect of the complex investment decisions facing an industrial firm. It is also perceived today that OPT provides the best and most economically consistent set of quantitative tools for capturing complex interactions of time and uncertainty inherent in investment decisions.

Significant industrial applications of OPT cover a very broad range of subjects. They include the evaluation of research and development projects, natural resource exploration, flexible production facilities, and optimal timing and abandonment decisions, to cite just a few. The analytical techniques involved in OPT require the use of stochastic calculus and general equilibrium pricing methods of financial economics. A continuous lognormal diffusion process, sometimes superimposed on a Poisson or jump process, is commonly used to model uncertainty.

At General Motors (GM), OPT has been successfully applied to capital investment decisions involving new manufacturing technologies, new product introduction, and flexible plant capacity. More specifically, it has been used as a financial tool to evaluate developmental activities for new technologies that would require sequential capital investments. Investment at each stage was modeled as buying an option to invest in the next stage. Implementing this approach explicitly takes into account the value of the upside potential of a new product or technology. In addition, OPT was instrumental in generating significant insights about investment in flexible plant capacity. It helped calculate the dollar value of the flexibility to quickly accommodate demand levels for different products exceeding the dedicated capacity of a manufacturing facility. It also helped to compute the dollar value of the flexibility to increase the volume of a product that turns out to be more profitable than originally expected. An important result from the application of OPT at GM has been the realization that there is an optimal level of product-mix flexibility, beyond which any additional benefits are marginal. Consequently, only a certain percentage of total capacity has to support flexible manufacturing. Recent extensions of the technique provide significant assistance in evaluating international projects by explicitly taking into account the impact of exchange rate volatility.

Financial executives in industry have indicated the importance of using OPT to evaluate their most complex investment decisions. Other companies, such as Merck and Company, GTE Laboratories, and McKinsey and Company, have also used OPT in their planning. (See [10], [11], and [12].)

There is a great need today to translate business strategies into consistent capital allocation decisions. OPT provides the quantitative background that can, in principle, fulfill this need. The analytical tools that result from continuing research in this area would significantly contribute to making more informed investment decisions (see Figure 3.1.)

3.2   Simulation and Design—Aircraft

The design of aircraft is unusual as an engineering discipline in several respects. The degree of dominance of computational and mathematical modeling in the design process is rare. The importance of successful design to the competitive viability of the product is unusual, as is the rate of technical progress and innovation. The high degree of cooperation among industry, government, and academia is no doubt important for the rate of progress; so is the level of governmental support for the development of the fundamental science. The computationally intensive aspect of the design process probably increased the rate of technical innovation as well.

The importance of design is easy to understand. The rate of fuel consumption is largely independent of speed through much of the tran-

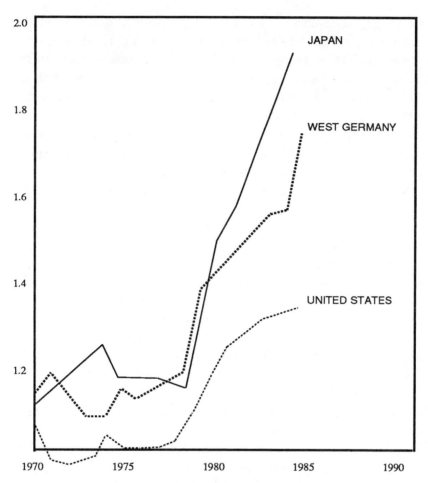

FIGURE 3.1 Industrial-funded R&D as a percentage of gross domestic product. Surveys reveal that high priority is attached to return on investment for U.S. managers, and to market share for Japanese managers. Cost accounting, which neglects the option value of investments, leads to systematic undervaluation of research and to short time horizons. Whether for these or other reasons, the results of the last decade show a consistently lower rate of investment in R&D by U.S. managers than by their Japanese and German counterparts. Reprinted, by permission, from [4]. Copyright ©1989 by MIT Press.

sonic range. The design goal is to fly subsonic, but only slightly so, and the design problem is to find the wing and total aircraft shapes that are efficient at these speeds. For example, an increase in speed of 10 percent allows a decrease in fuel costs of 10 percent, but through better utilization of the fleet of aircraft, a reduction of all operating and capital costs by about 10 percent is achieved as well. These reduced costs, in turn, determine the competitive viability of the aircraft, and averaged over the useful life of the fleet to which the design applies, far outweigh any conceivable level of design costs.

Early successful computer design algorithms were developed in collaboration between mathematicians and aeronautical engineers, and for reasons given above, considerable effort has gone into improving the computations and the modeling since then. Computations have replaced a large fraction of the expensive and time-consuming tests done in wind tunnels. More importantly, based on computational fluid dynamics, far greater ranges of tests can now be carried out in wind tunnels. Manufacturers of commercial aircraft use computer modeling to obtain certificates of airworthiness for new aircraft designs more quickly than would otherwise be possible. Because of their efficiency and lower cost, computations allow consideration of an increased range of design alternatives and thus lead to an increased quality of design. The computational approach also shortens the duration of the design cycle, an important aspect of economic competitiveness. Because the most important part of the fluid flow field is near the wing, the computations are arranged to consider this region more carefully, through the use of adaptive grids. A substantial effort goes into the construction of grids alone. Another large effort has been mounted to improve the computational algorithms that describe the fluid dynamics. Turbulence modeling is important because even the fastest computers do not resolve all the physically important phenomena, especially in the boundary layer near the wing surface. Thus, approximate descriptions of the phenomena are required. Flame chemistry and combustion are important within the jet turbine. The turbulent flow behind the wing is a safety hazard for closely following aircraft since the trailing vortex remains stable for relatively long times. That fact has to be considered in determining the safe spacing of aircraft—not only for takeoffs and landings, but in the air traffic corridors as well. Vortex methods have been applied to this problem; they produce very highly resolved portraits of the flow field. All of the above areas are currently undergoing active research; the results of this research will be needed for the next aircraft design cycle (see Figure 3.2).

Structural strength and stability are modeled through the use of finite element codes, while wing flutter analysis is an eigenvalue problem. Composite materials are used in aircraft design, for example, to produce strong but flexible helicopter blades. Mathematical theories of homogenization are used to describe the material strength of such composites. The significance of control for aircraft lies in the fact that there are more mechanical degrees of freedom available to the designer than can be used effectively by the pilot. Control theory allows selection of optimal control parameters, for the pilot's use. Fluid dynamic simulation codes can predict the effect of control surfaces on the flight response, and thus apply not only to cruise conditions, but also to the transient conditions of takeoff and landing. One aspect of pilot training, and therefore public safety, is the pilot's ability to respond to emergency conditions. The operation of an aircraft in adverse conditions can obviously be studied only by computer simulation. Pilot training in unusual conditions (landing with some engines not working, for example) can then be obtained in a computer-operated flight simulator. The flight simulator, of necessity, is instructed by the computational simulation of fluid dynamics.

3.3 Design and Control of Complex Systems

The mathematical sciences have played a major role in the development of the engineering capabilities required to design and control high-performance systems. Mathematical models have become a standard part of the preliminary design process for building such systems. They are the building blocks on which virtually all computer-aided design (CAD) software is based. These models are significantly less expensive to build and run, in terms of both time and money, than more traditional physical prototypes. Mathematical models are especially useful either when a proposed design is to be tested for feasibility or when the number of degrees of freedom is so large that guidance is necessary to reduce the range of design or control choices. In a semiconductor wafer fabrication facility, for instance, the manufacturing process may

38

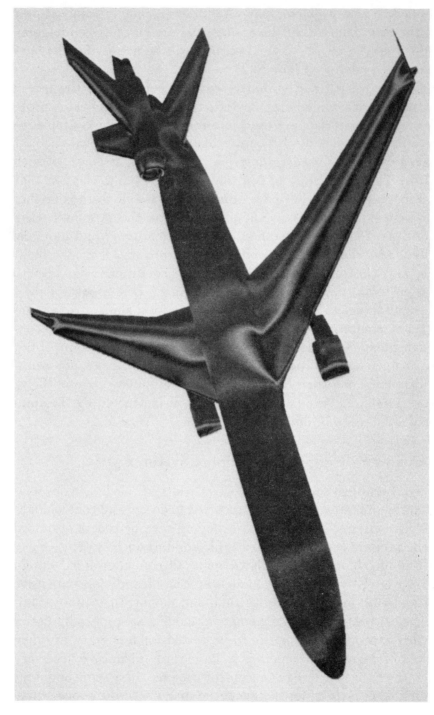

FIGURE 3.2 Flow past a McDonnell-Douglas MDC Trijet at Mach number 0.825 and an angle of attack of 2.50 degrees. The contours indicate surface pressure; the lighter shade shows the low pressure in the hypersonic regime. Courtesy of McDonnell-Douglas Aircraft Co., Long Beach, Calif.

consist of hundreds of steps, each of which can be modified somewhat in order to improve the yield in high-quality chips. An engineer using mathematical modeling quickly gains an understanding of the basic qualitative behavior of the system (e.g., how the system responds to an increase in the load on some subsystem). This deeper insight into system behavior can have an important impact on the ultimate quality of the design produced. Finally, the development of real-time control strategies for these systems inherently relies on mathematical and computational tools and representations, since the system typically must respond without human intervention.

The engineering systems being designed and built today involve systems issues of a complexity that would have been difficult to imagine even two decades ago. This point is perhaps best illustrated with examples.

1. With the advent of computer-integrated manufacturing, the hardware capabilities of modern manufacturing systems are constantly increasing. However, it frequently turns out that a significant bottleneck to full utilization of these sophisticated resources can be linked to the complex interactions among the various machines that make up the system. For example, it is well known that the manner in which orders are released through a multi-product manufacturing facility can have a major impact on the throughput of the system. Machine interference can occur when orders are improperly scheduled, which can significantly affect the productivity of the facility.

The "intelligence" of modern manufacturing systems, in which mathematical theory augments conventional engineering, creates new opportunities for system control that were not present in the previous technologies. The information gathering and processing capability of current systems permits the facility to monitor quality problems in real time and to deal with local bottlenecks by rescheduling orders appropriately.

2. Consider the nation's long-distance telephone network as it exists today. The overwhelming amount of traffic carried by the nation's long-distance telephone network is voice. The traffic is digitized and carried in a communication mode called circuit-switching. For circuit-switching, the call is given its circuits at set-up time for its exclusive use; i.e., no sharing or buffering is involved. An alternative approach,

called packet-switching, is built on the premise that buffering (in units called packets) leads to more efficient use of bandwidth, especially for sporadic traffic with bursts of high volume. Data traffic generated by computers and terminals has such characteristics, and data networks and services are being used increasingly. A great deal of research, much of it mathematical, is being focused on the design of wide-area data networks operating at very high speeds, i.e., at gigabits per second. The National Research and Educational Network, with its goal of linking 3,000 campuses, represents a milestone in national networking.

Modeling these systems as networks of queues abstracts mathematically the basic structure present in these examples. Each resource (e.g., the node-to-node "links" in the long-distance network, the input-output devices in a computer system, the work centers in a manufacturing facility) in the system is modeled as a queue with a waiting room and an associated set of servers. Customers (e.g., packets in the network setting, requests to a data base, orders in a manufacturing facility) move from queue to queue as service is received from each facility along a customer's path. Congestion occurs in the model when large numbers of customers contend for limited resources. The degree of congestion has an important impact on the performance of the system. As a consequence, systems designers often use these models to determine the "choke points" of their systems. The system can then be reconfigured by the designer to mitigate the impact of these "choke points."

The arrival and service time patterns of customers in these models are unpredictable, and therefore, probability theory and statistics play a large role. If certain special assumptions are made about the nature of the patterns of unpredictability, then key performance measures can be calculated in terms of the solution of a (very large) system of simultaneous linear equations. Thus, significant effort has been expended in recent years to develop computational algorithms capable of solving these large systems of equations.

Frequently, the system of linear equations is so large that conventional numerical techniques are inapplicable. Fortunately, a large class of queuing networks has a product-form structure. The product-form structure permits one to calculate the performance measures of interest by solving a much smaller system of linear equations. The development, analysis, and extension of the product-form queuing network theory have had a significant impact on the performance of complex engineering systems. Similar product-form equations arise in mathematical models of human physiology. Software packages that make significant use of these modeling ideas are fundamentally altering the culture of the engineering community. They offer design engineers rapid preliminary analysis and feasibility studies for systems of a complexity that would be difficult, if not impossible, to attack using other techniques.

The mathematical sciences have also made decisive contributions to the study of the real-time control issues associated with these complex systems. Based on an interplay between exact solutions of simple models and educated guesses for realistic situations checked by performance analysis, effective decision rules can be found. This approach to developing control rules for real-time applications has met with success in manufacturing contexts (e.g., reducing the scrap rate when using computer-controlled lathes to cut metal), as well as telecommunications settings (e.g., dynamic routing of packets in digital networks).

Simulations are used in situations in which analysis is too difficult to be tractable or enlightening. Discrete-event simulation is a methodology that mathematical scientists have played a leading role in developing. The discrete events are, for example, customers propagating from one station to another in a queuing network, with states that change discretely (rather than continuously). The computer simulation approach offers the system designer an opportunity to visualize the actual operation of the system over time (e.g., in a manufacturing setting, one can watch parts being assembled as they travel through the facility). As a consequence, many commercially available simulation packages have extensive graphical interfacing capabilities. A disadvantage of simulation, relative to the more limited tools described above, is that building simulation models typically requires considerably more development effort on the part of the systems designer (in part because a simulation usually models the system at a higher level of detail). A research topic of great interest is the design of algorithms for discrete-event simulations that harness the power of large numbers of processors (several thousand in the Connection Machine) in massively parallel computers.

3.4   Machine Tools for Manufacturing

According to reliable estimates, the United States spends over $100 billion each year in machining operations. Industrial efforts to reduce these costs involve development of new and improved materials for cutting tools. The most advanced tools are made of ceramic composites. Knowledge concerning the characteristics of these composites, such as their extreme hardness, corrosion and wear resistance, strength at elevated temperatures, and electrical properties, comes from physical experiments. These experiments are very complex because they involve a large number of intricately linked variables, and the interrelations among the variables may not be known. The experiments are subject to the sensitivity of the processes, to uncontrollable processing variations, and to unavoidable variations in raw materials. The techniques of statistically planned experiments that have been developed over the last 50 years are particularly useful to address such situations. Such techniques were applied to the problem of ceramic composites processing research, in a collaboration involving materials scientists, statisticians, and an industrial ceramics developer.

The focus of the collaboration was processing of silicon carbide whisker reinforced alumina matrix composites used as advanced cutting tools. The object of the experiment was to study the cause-and-effect relationships among processing conditions (whisker characteristics and amount, time, temperature, and pressure), microstructures (density, alumina grain size, and homogeneity), mechanical properties (flexural strength, hardness, and fracture toughness), and machining performance (flank and nose wear). The results of a set of experiments indicated that hardness and strength are strong indicators of machining performance, and mean density is a strong predictor of hardness and strength. In addition, robust processing conditions applicable to the kind of equipment used were identified. The fractional factorial experiment approach used in this study reduced the cost of conducting the experiment by a factor of four without sacrificing any relevant information. The key idea is to consider the multidimensional space defined by the input factors and to focus on evaluating only the linear effects (main effects) and pairwise interaction effects of the input factors on the output responses. The benefits of such collaborative research accrue when efficient strategies, based on factorial experiments and other designs, are routinely used by experimental scientists and engineers in the design and optimization of the materials processing conditions.

3.5 Simulation and Production—Petroleum

The mathematical sciences play a central role in many aspects of the development of our energy potential from hydrocarbons. The same techniques are applicable to other problems of national interest. Applications to groundwater flow, contaminant transport, cleanup of hazardous waste, and nuclear waste disposal all require the same mathematical and computational techniques. Applied mathematicians, numerical analysts, and computational scientists are becoming essential components of groups addressing such problems in many applications.

Mathematical models are important in exploration for petroleum, in characterizing the reservoirs, geologically and geochemically, and in developing production strategies to optimize recovery. The following physical problems have been studied systematically by mathematical scientists: building correct mathematical models from physical principles; understanding the mathematical properties of the models, such as existence, uniqueness, regularity, and continuous dependence of the solution upon data; developing discretization methods in a stable and accurate fashion; and producing computational algorithms, which take advantage of the emerging computer architectures for efficient solution.

Exploration via seismic inverse techniques leads to an extremely difficult mathematical problem. This is the inverse problem, in which a portion of the solution is given (the source signal and the reflected signal at sensor locations on the earth's surface), and the problem is to find the equation generating the solution, i.e., the reflection and transmission coefficients of the deeply buried geological layers. The direct problem is linear, but the inverse problem is highly nonlinear. Since uniqueness and continuous dependence of the solution (i.e., the geology) on data (i.e., the seismic signal) are properties that are almost impossible to attain, there is a need to quantify the degree of nonuniqueness, to deal with noisy data, and to identify new data collection locations and techniques to decrease the ill-posedness of the problem. Analysis of shear waves and elastic response has recently been included in seismic interpretation. Accurate interface conditions, absorbing boundary conditions, and grid refinement techniques are sorely needed for three-dimensional applications. Finally, efficient solution algorithms, which take advantage of the new parallel and vector computer architectures, must be developed for full three-dimensional seismic problems.

Large-scale models of basin evolution provide a more global approach to locating oil deposits and discovering properties of petroleum reservoirs. The basin models describe thermal maturation, geochemical diagenesis, and local fluid flow effects over geological time periods. These models incorporate descriptions of processes from macroscopic plate tectonics to microscopic pore and throat development and geochemical changes. Large, coupled systems of nonlinear partial differential equations describe these complex geological, geochemical, and geothermal processes. These techniques, coupled with sedimentary and depositional theories, are essential in the location of subtle stratigraphic traps. They also form the basis of reservoir characterization in general. Advancement in these areas is being seriously impeded by the need for mathematics at all levels—from existence/uniqueness theorems to large-scale algorithm development. Geostatistics and length-scale averaging via homogenization techniques are also very important for dealing with uncertainty in the data.

Since primary and secondary recovery techniques leave up to 70 percent of the original oil in place, improved oil recovery methods are necessary so that we may use this major domestic source of energy. Large-scale reservoir simulation is essential as a predictive mechanism to help understand the fluid, physical, and chemical processes and use them to optimize hydrocarbon production. Present simulation techniques cause a serious loss of detail of the flow description and thus give limited, but still valuable, information. Compositional paths and Riemann problems have been studied by both engineers and mathematicians to provide insight into nonlinear wave and frontal interactions. A recent analysis of three-phase flow equations has revealed nonphysical features in commonly used equations, leading to a revision of the equations used in large-scale simulations. There is a need for better numerical techniques in large-scale simulation to resolve complex local physical phenomena.

Reservoir fluid flow should be studied in collaboration with geologists, geochemists, and geostatisticians to develop better reservoir characterizations and to incorporate data on different length scales in the simulators. For fractured reservoirs, a dual system of equations exists: for flow in the fracture cracks and for flow in the rock matrix between the cracks. The coupling between these systems depends on the spacing between the cracks as well as the detailed properties of the rock matrix. This coupling has been studied recently, using homogenization theory. Interface methods follow the fluid interfaces, and adaptive grid refinement methods resolve the local physics of the complex chemical and physical fluid interactions. The nonlinear fingering process must be understood in the context of reservoir heterogeneities. Also, the global effects of the fingering process must be modeled on a reservoir scale, since this phenomenon will often dominate the flooding process. Usually this modeling is done by homogenization methods. The highly nonlinear, coupled systems of partial differential equations required in the models of enhanced oil recovery processes must be analyzed to obtain their major properties. Extremely difficult, large-scale inverse problems are necessary for history matching to obtain the unknown reservoir and flow properties in situ. Mixed finite-element methods, characteristic methods, and upwind methods give improved discretization techniques for the accurate treatment of nonlinear, transport-dominated flows. Due to the enormous size of the problems for field-scale applications, efficiency is the key to success, and algorithm development must use the newly emerging capabilities of supercomputers. Preliminary indications are that parallel computing will succeed in resolving the reservoir simulation problem.

3.6 Statistical Quality Control and Improvement

Statistics has very widespread applications and is among the leaders of the mathematical sciences in this regard. Statistics gains its importance in the physical and engineering sciences through the interpretation of measurements and the analysis of statistical significance and of errors in field and laboratory data. The use of statistics is well established in the biological sciences and medicine. In the social sciences, statistics is fundamental. Often statistics is the first of the mathematical sciences used in the analysis of data, and the first to be actively involved in the mathematical formulation of new science or technology, as the necessary precursor to its quantitative evolution.

The use of statistics for quality control originated from the need to control complex manufacturing operations. In order to meet this demand, a number of new statistical ideas were formed and developed. Sequential sampling provides a notable example of the far-reaching effects that resulted. Sequential sampling has been used in the conduct and analysis of drug studies and clinical trials. At the same time, the emphasis on collecting data and applying basic and standard statistical techniques was highly successful in improving quality and reducing costs.

Statistically planned experiments were, in the main, developed within the context of agricultural experimentation. These methods have had phenomenal success in increasing crop yields and animal production. The ability of these strategies to extract vital information from comparatively few experiments is of great value, especially in manufacturing.

It is now commonplace to have mechanical design questions treated through carefully planned experiments. Influenced largely by the design engineer G. Taguchi, the focus of many experiments is on the reduction of variability of the performance of a product—now recognized as a key component of quality. Traditional statistical approaches were not clearly appropriate for such a goal. New statistical problems were formulated, leading to new experimental strategies and analyses. This is an area of ongoing research.

The following two case studies describe applications of statistical quality control (SQC) to problems in AT&T manufacturing units. These examples illustrate that substantial quality improvements (and consistent cost savings) result from the application of SQC to manufacturing processes.

In one example of a new automatic assembly, an operation comprising two assembly machines was plagued by low productivity: one machine was operating at 50 percent of its design capacity whereas the other was operating at only 25 percent of its design capacity. Despite numerous problems, no data had been collected.

The first activity of the SQC investigation was to collect data to identify the failure modes. Using standard techniques, the SQC team identified the principal problem: too great a variability in the dimensions of plastic parts used in the assembly. A related problem was excess bowing and warping in these parts caused by excessive variability in the melting point of the plastic from one batch to another owing to overly generous specifications. The machines were simply insufficiently robust to tolerate such variability. The solution was (1) to reduce variability in the dimensions of the plastic components and (2) to increase the robustness of the machines.

A secondary problem was excessive variability of the solder coating of certain metal components used in the process: on occasion, the coating was too thick and the component jammed. On investigation, it was discovered that the variability of the coating was within design specifications, but the latter were, again, overly generous. The problem was solved by adjusting the machine to permit greater variability and by tightening the specification.

After a year's work, the productivity increased by 121 percent, the labor hours were cut by 61 percent, and the yield (proportion of usable products) increased from 90 percent to 98 percent.

A second example concerned serious problems in the manufacture of an electronic component: the yield was only 84 percent, and only 50 percent of the scheduled delivery dates were met. A major difficulty was excess variability of the various characteristics of the component assembly. Variability occurred particularly in the automatically controlled acid bath used in the manufacture. SQC techniques identified the problem: the machinery that determined the pH value of the acid and corrected any discrepancies was overcompensating, causing excess variability. Reducing this variability by recalibration increased the yield to 95 percent. Additional problems caused by excess variability in constituent parts were also corrected by imposing tighter controls.

In the first year of operation after these corrections, $12 million was saved and the proportion of delivery dates met increased to 95 percent.

3.7 Manufacturing Process Control

Continuous production control is vital in the metals, glass, and chemical industries, among others. Process control in these applications typically involves 20 to 200 control variables and 10 to 100 quality (response) variables. The objective of the control is to monitor and adjust the process to ensure that the quality measures of the products meet the specifications of the customers. A basic difficulty in such control problems is that the information available for relating control and quality variables is typically obtained during product manufacture, and thus is observational in character. Designed experiments are extremely difficult to carry out, owing to the very large number of control variables and the practical difficulties of perturbing a large-scale industrial process.

Process improvement calls for (1) sophisticated methods of variable selection to discover the most influential control variables and (2) high-dimensional nonlinear modeling to approximate their effect on the quality measures. These procedures can require massive computational resources, multivariate methods for time series data, and graphical representation and modeling of high-dimensional data.

Major management goals in the control of manufacturing processes include the discovery of better methods of process diagnosis and the development of effective procedures for quality improvement. The first goal requires the identification of quality variables specifically sensitive to particular steps in the process or particular pieces of equipment that may be drifting out of control. The second goal requires the development of a high-dimensional model, presumably nonlinear, that quantifies the effect of changes in the values of the control variables on the quality variables.

The large number of control variables means that the statistical analysis is operating at the very edge of what is currently possible and requires the development of new experimental procedures. Fortunately, there is some prior information that can be used to sharpen the analysis. Industry engineers have scientific grounds for believing that the response surface will be relatively flat with respect to most of the control variables and most interactions. Also, again on physical grounds, there is often an understanding of the functional form of the relationship between some of the control and quality variables.

A manufacturing process vital to U.S. economic competitiveness is the fabrication of very large scale integrated (VLSI) circuits or computer chips. This specific example illustrates some of the points made above. The process is extremely complex and is becoming much more so as the density of devices on the chips continues to increase dramatically. As this density increases, the process tolerances are decreased, and process control becomes more sensitive, so that statistical methods are of ever increasing importance. The development of statistical methods to understand this process better, to diagnose equipment malfunctions, to increase yield, and to reduce process variability represents a major technical challenge.

The VLSI fabrication process consists of several steps performed on silicon wafers. The steps include oxidation, photolithography, plasma etching, and so on. Some of these steps are repeated many times over the course of the fabrication process. Determination of whether an integrated circuit (IC) produced by this process will be acceptable depends on several characteristics measured at the completion of the process (e.g., zero state threshold voltage, V_{T0}). If a characteristic is not acceptable, the defect may have occurred at any one of several early steps in the process. Unfortunately, one cannot measure characteristics such as V_{T0} until fabrication is completed. The proportion of unacceptable ICs is often quite high for a new product, until the processes involved are stabilized.

It would be useful to model the steps in the VLSI fabrication process, statistically, in order to be able to monitor and adjust the quality of ICs as they are being produced, and to detect equipment malfunctions at the end of a process step rather than at the end of the entire fabrication process.

3.8   Sensor-Based Manufacturing

Modern control theory has shown in the aerospace industry that dramatic improvements can be achieved by using all available sensors. The United States is the world leader in the areas of control and signal processing (e.g., Kalman filtering, adaptive filtering, unsupervised learning, iterative deconvolution) required for optimal extraction of information from sensor data. Much of this work has been carried out by mathematically inclined engineers, drawing on a broad range of mathematical disciplines. Preliminary investigation has demonstrated that application of these ideas to the field of semiconductor fabrication can have a significant impact on process performance. Furthermore, with a projected cost of \$1 billion for an IC fabrication line in the year 2000, a reduction in start-up time and defect percentages can have a tremendous financial impact.

Lithography is a key process in IC manufacturing: it involves the generation of masks, and the attendant problems in their use. A common estimate is that nearly three-fourths of the manufacturing costs of semiconductor chips can be attributed to the lithography stage. Among the problems in lithography are the methods for measuring critical dimensions (e.g., linewidths) rapidly and noninvasively. Recently neural network classification strategies have been applied to edge detection of wafer patterns using digitized images. Successful results have been confirmed in several test cases by careful comparison to time-consuming measurements obtained by use of a scanning electron microscope. The neural network algorithms are noninvasive and rapid, and they have low noise sensitivity because of an adaptation mechanism. Furthermore, the unsupervised neural network device requires only normally available a priori information and can also be applied to solve the problem of mask-wafer alignment. More generally, a number of digital image processing techniques that have been used so successfully for satellite and space-probe images could be used in lithography; the barriers between fields are such that lithographers have focused more on direct physical measurement as opposed to indirect measurement followed by signal processing.

A recent application in this direction has been to new methods for temperature measurement of wafers being processed in very hot (1000°C) rapid thermal processing ovens. Pyrometers are relatively inexpensive temperature measuring devices but their accuracy is poor. Therefore, there is a considerable research effort to devise sensors based on other principles. However, by using appropriate signal processing techniques (in particular, a type of extended Kalman filtering technique), it appears that the pyrometer measurements can be processed to yield accurate temperature measurements and to track their variation with time.

Such temperature measurements are currently used by semiconductor specialists to gauge the progress of various reactions and processes. However, they are also essential in the application of modern multivariate control strategies, which when given the measurements of a reasonable number of sensor variables and given a reasonable number of control parameters, can give significantly better control than that achievable with single variable controls. Through the use of computers and signal processing strategies, the mathematical models on which the control is based can be updated with the acquisition of new data, to optimize manufacturing operations or paths to improve quality and throughput.

3.9 Manufacturing Standards

The highly competitive IC industry has a never-ending demand for submicrometer feature sizes on ICs and for metrological techniques for measuring and characterizing these features. Early on, the IC industry became aware that there was a problem in obtaining agreement of linewidth measurements among the mask suppliers and IC manufacturers. The National Institute of Standards and Technology (NIST), an agency in the U.S. Department of Commerce, was asked by a commercial standards maker to check its linewidth measurement standards. The absence of standards at the required dimensions had led to a proliferation of industrial in-house standards with no agreement among them.

The fundamental problem was identified as the measurement of the width of the lines on the IC photomask. A decision was made to create a new measurement reference, an artifact that mimicked the photomasks used in industry. A measurement system was developed, interactions between the measurement instrument and the specimen were studied, procedures for properly using the photomask in the field were developed, and theoretical models were developed to explain how an optical microscope would respond to light diffracting around the edges of a line on the photomask.

Establishing control in manufacturing across numerous industrial suppliers and consumers requires a process metrology that is consistent across all users. Such a process metrology is based on modeling and experimentation found in modern statistical theory and practice. Two elements of this modeling and experimentation stand out: (1) so-called round-robin experiments across industrial sites to establish precise measures of variation from site to site and (2) individual measurement control systems at a site that enable the continuous improvement of measurement quality. Mathematical techniques of efficient experimentation and measurement process control are fundamental to establishing these elements.

The round-robin experiment required a high-precision test specimen, which was developed by NIST. The round-robin, involving 10 companies (IC manufacturers, photomask makers, and instrument makers), clearly demonstrated that there was a measurement problem in the industry. Following this experiment, NIST developed its first linewidth standard. A procedure was developed by NIST statisticians to ensure measurement process control for the certification of each standard reference material (SRM) issued for sale to the IC industry. These certified standards were immediately in great demand. Linewidth standards are now available for a number of materials. An automated measurement system and sophisticated statistical process control procedures are used to certify the linewidths on these photomasks. These standards are in demand and many manufacturing firms have adopted this technology.

This example illustrates the use of SRMs. These are well-characterized, homogeneous, stable materials with specific properties that are measured and certified by a national reference laboratory. An extensive campaign of measurements and tests is undertaken during the process of developing and certifying SRMs, and collaboration of statisticians with the physical scientists who actually make the measurements plays an essential role. The composition of 90 percent of the steel produced in the United States is controlled by measurements based on SRMs. SRMs serve nearly all sectors of manufacturing, including electronics, instruments, computer instrumentation, ferrous and nonferrous metals, mining, glass, rubber, plastics, primary chemicals, nuclear power, and transportation.

3.10   Production, Inventories, and Marketing

Equipment acquisition and purchased subassemblies account for more than 90 percent of the manufacturing costs of some high-technology products. Many companies avoid corresponding increases in the costs of capital by more carefully coordinating their production, inventories, and product distribution. Their efforts combine statistical data analysis and operations research methods.

Pfizer, Inc., one of the country's major pharmaceutical manufacturers, reduced its U.S. inventories by $24 million during a three-year period, improved its customer service by reducing its back orders by 95 percent, and sharply improved overall management control. Five years of production and sales history were statistically analyzed to develop mathematical models for production lot sizes and target inventory levels. The models were optimized with a combination of dynamic programming and artificial intelligence techniques.

Net interest expenses for Blue Bell, Inc., one of the world's largest apparel manufacturers, had increased 20-fold. Financing inventory had dramatically pushed up the company's cost of doing business. A new production planning process, designed with operations research techniques and statistical data analysis, was tested and implemented. In less than two years, inventories were reduced by $115 million with neither a decrease in sales or customer service, nor an increase in other manufacturing costs.

Bethlehem Steel is the second largest U.S. steel producer. It faced the challenge of efficiently operating a new ingot mold stripping facility against strong competition. The competing process had the disadvantage of higher capital costs, but the advantage of improved yield, productivity, and product quality. Optimization of the ingot-based plant utilized combinatorial mathematics and mathematical programming to select ingot mold sizes. The resulting annual savings exceeded $8 million.

The cost of financing working capital at CITGO, the nation's largest independent refiner and marketer of petroleum products, had increased more than 30-fold while gross margins had decreased. An optimization-based decision support system for planning supply, distribution, and marketing (called the SDM system) was developed and implemented. The system, based in large part on statistics and mathematical programming, integrates CITGO's key economic and physical SDM characteristics over a short-term (11-week) planning horizon. Management uses the system for many types of decision making—pricing; where to buy, sell, or trade products; how much inventory to maintain; and how much product to ship by which method. Major benefits accruing from the SDM model included reduction in product inventory and improved operational decision making. Annual interest savings of $14 million were realized after an inventory reduction of $116 million. Improvements in decision making are estimated to be worth another $25 million yearly.

3.11 Maintenance and Repair

Mathematical and statistical modeling and simulation are vital steps in the process of planning viable repair and maintenance facilities, especially if the facilities are complex, involving multiple work stations, sources of supplies, and so on. The same considerations apply as well to the design of manufacturing facilities. The initial consideration is feasibility: will the proposed facility function well, in terms of costs, inventory, and production cycle time? Once feasibility is established, simulations provide invaluable information regarding facility design, deployment, and use of machinery, parts, and personnel. After an optimally designed facility has been built, further simulations allow final adjustment of operating procedures to achieve optimal performance.

Consider the case of United Airlines, faced with the problem of turbine blade repair. Although the general image of aircraft repair may be one of mechanics swarming over planes, in what constitutes a job shop approach, in actuality there may be significant cost savings in establishing specialized facilities to "remanufacture" certain standard parts. United decided to establish such a dedicated facility to remanufacture turbine blades. The facility was expected to cost $15 million. An initial feasibility study was undertaken to determine whether the dedicated facility would function better than the job shop in terms of costs, inventory, and repair cycle time. The simulations were based on probability models for distributions of demand for repaired blades, supplies of defective blades, and the progression of repair through the remanufacturing stages of the facility. Once feasibility was established, simulations allowed optimal balance of all production and repair machinery. After the construction of this optimally designed facility, the actual operation gave rise to additional data in terms of revised probability measures in the simulation model, which allowed further simulations, to achieve improved performance.

The economic leverage of these simulations is considerable, as a small investment in simulation can save many hundreds of thousands of dollars on a project of the size discussed above.

4 THE TECHNOLOGY BASE

A leading economic competitiveness issue pertaining to the mathematical sciences is technology transfer. The record is uneven, with technology transfer flourishing on some occasions and languishing on others. Technology transfer is an area of professional activity largely lacking in visibility, and for this reason, some of its successes are documented in this report. Also included is the history of one prominent failure of technology transfer.

Economic competitiveness, among other factors, requires a broad technology base from which to derive new methods of production, quantitative information (data) and analysis, and quality control methodology.

In this chapter, numerous examples show how the mathematical sciences have contributed to that technology base and helped to make possible the manufacture of new or improved goods, or the offering of a new or better service. In doing so, it is emphasized that the distinction between direct and indirect support, and between short- and long-range connections, cannot be drawn in a clear fashion. Consider the example of weather forecasts, clearly and naturally a part of the technology infrastructure. The forecasts depend on computer simulations and mathematical modeling, and thus derive in part from the mathematical sciences. Forecasts of wind currents and jet stream location are used in flight planning for commercial aircraft, and are as important a contributor to fuel economy as is the design of advanced wing foils (cited in §3.2). Forecasts are used by fishing fleets in deciding whether to extend their nets. Knowledge of the probability of precipitation is used by farmers in harvest planning. Prediction of severe weather patterns is used in planning to minimize losses from high winds and from flooding due to high tides. Forecasts of temperature and humidity are used to minimize the economic cost and maximize the benefits of complying with environmental air quality regulations. From this example of weather forecasts, it becomes evident that there is not a sharp distinction between the technology base and direct applications.

The following discussion of the technology base does not focus narrowly on modeling and simulation. There is a fundamental significance to the mathematical way of thinking. Briefly, mathematics provides methods for organizing and structuring knowledge so that, when applied to technology, it allows scientists and engineers to produce systematic, reproducible, and transmittable knowledge. Analysis, design, modeling, simulation, and implementation then become possible as efficient, well-structured activities.

Similarly, the distinction between short- and long-term applications cannot be drawn unambiguously. In a series of cases, one finds the same subjects moving back and forth between theory and applications, and becoming richer with each transition, as the following examples illustrate:

- Nearly integrable systems of differential equations and fiber optics;

- Geometrical optics and the asymptotic solutions of differential equations;

- Fourier analysis, group symmetries, and special functions;

- Covariant differential geometry and elastic deformations; and

- Fourier analysis on finite groups and the fast-Fourier-transform (FFT) algorithm.

The ability of the mathematical sciences to deliver short-term results with any degree of consistency depends crucially on support for their long-term development. Conversely, the more fundamental areas of the mathematical sciences are continually invigorated by interaction with applications. It is an almost universal experience that once an application succeeds, further progress depends on the development of new, and often fundamental, theories. This report endorses the principle that short-term applications and fundamental theories are virtually inseparable. It does not attempt to make narrow distinctions within the technology base. Rather, the point of this chapter is to analyze areas of the mathematical sciences and to document their close connection to economic competitiveness, thereby establishing the importance of the technology base.

4.1 Technology Transfer

The technology transfer of importance to this report is the transfer of ideas, methods, and results from the mathematical sciences community to engineering and industrial groups for the purpose of improving the technical operation and economic competitiveness of U.S. industry. In view of the continuous web of ideas and values that make up the intellectual life of our nation, it seems most practical to promote the transfer of technology broadly to all segments of the economy, even though the concerns of this report relate most directly to support of the manufacturing sector.

Technology transfer is not usually recognized as an area of mathematics, and for this reason it is generally lacking in visibility. It is included here because of its importance to economic competitiveness and because mathematical scientists have extensive activities in this area. There are serious problems with technology transfer, problems that are by no means confined to the mathematical sciences alone. Unfortunately, the time required for transfer is long, commonly spanning one or more decades.

Historically, the transfer of technology from the statistical design of experiments to quality improvement in manufacturing has followed a tortuous path. In the 1920s, the British statistician and geneticist R. A. Fisher led the development of statistical theory and methods for experimentation. Fisher was stimulated largely by agricultural applications, and his ideas were rapidly adopted there and became extraordinarily successful.

Statisticians realized that these ideas also applied in industrial contexts. Statistical methods for experimental design were used by Tippett to improve productivity in the cotton and woolen industries in England, starting in the mid-1920s. Transfer of these ideas to manufacturing took place subsequently, but on a limited scale, largely confined to the chemical and pharmaceutical industries. Also, during the 1920s, the foundations of statistical quality control were established at AT&T, in an effort spearheaded by Shewhart. In the 1950s, Deming, strongly influenced by Shewhart and the power of statistical quality control, brought the message of quality to Japan. His influence on Japanese manufacturing, and notably on the Japanese engineer Taguchi, was profound and was an important reason for the success Japan has had in industrial competition. Taguchi's contribution was to adapt the experimental design methodology, developed earlier in the United Kingdom and the United States, to problems of reducing variability in the performance of products, thereby increasing their quality. Concerns about America's competitiveness in the 1980s has led to the transfer, through Taguchi, of the methods of statistically planned experiments into the design and manufacture of products in a number of American industries. The basic ideas have been available since the 1920s, as have the initial successful applications. The time scale for the transfer of this technology is not yet completed, but it already spans 70 years.

Some of the common causes of delay in the transfer of technology may include the following:

1. Need to refine technology. Is the user or the originator to work out the details? Turnkey technology is the easiest to transfer.

2. Evaluation. Which of the many new ideas would actually be beneficial to users?

3. Communication. Ideas expressed in the technical language of the user are more readily adopted.

4. Learning. Time is required to learn a new technology and to adapt it to a new situation.

5. Collective decision making. Often a consensus is required among users before a technology is tried or adopted. This reduces risk but does introduce delay.

6. Responsibility. For the transfer of technology to succeed, the responsibility for the transfer is normally assumed by the groups or individuals who discovered the technology. Usually an active effort is required to accomplish the transfer.

7. Necessity. Failure of old technology rather than the superiority of the new is often the critical step for adoption of new technology. Demonstration of failure may be time-consuming.

8. Not invented here. Users have a variety of real and imagined

reasons for resisting ideas from the outside.

9. Multiple layers. Often there is a chain of groups through which the ideas and technology must pass, including multiple academic disciplines, industrial service groups, and various industrial management groups.

It is also appropriate to examine the structural contexts in which technology transfer has occurred. Technology transfer between the mathematical sciences and industry is extensive, and is documented in the rest of this report. To be successful, technology transfer must carry information in both directions. The mathematical scientist learns as much as he or she teaches. Usually technology transfer works best when both parties share a common goal. It depends fundamentally on the establishment of working relationships and trust. A few systematic examples of technology transfer are noted below.

The Seminar on Industrial Problems[3] is held weekly at the Institute for Mathematics and its Applications (IMA) at the University of Minnesota. The speakers are from industry. The audience consists of IMA visitors and postdoctorates as well as graduate students and selected undergraduates from the University of Minnesota. The speakers present problems of a mathematical nature arising in their R&D activities. Subsequent to the presentation, there is usually a follow-up, and typically, within a period of several weeks to several months, many of the problems are partially or completely solved. Some of these problems lead to new and exciting mathematics. Here are a few examples considered by the Seminar on Industrial Problems.

1. Binary optics. Microelectronic techniques can be used to manufacture surfaces of optical substrates with stepped profile. Such optical devices can be used as lenses, avionic displays, and so on. The design

---

[3] *Industrial mathematics* is applicable mathematics that is used in an industrial context. It includes methods, tables, algorithms, modeling, and a feel for the magnitudes of relevant quantities. It includes large parts of applied mathematics, but does not include applications of mathematics to basic science, such as astrophysics and biology (other than biotechnology). *Applied mathematics* is a research field that develops and uses new or existing mathematical theory to solve problems of importance to society. Included in this field are solution methods, approximation methods, computer algorithms, and modeling. Because of the widespread applicability of mathematics, substantial portions of pure mathematics are included as well.

of the surface can be produced as software, but this step requires solving the Maxwell equations in the entire space with the surface to be designed as an interface between two optical media. Since the stepped profile does have corners, serious problems arise in trying to adapt traditional codes. An IMA team has found a new approach to solving the Maxwell equations, which leads to a very promising numerical method.

2. Electrophotography. Electrophotography is a process in which pictures are made of light and electricity. The common example is photocopying documents. One of the steps involved is creating a visual image from the electric image. Here the toner (ink) accumulates near the electric image of the dark spots of the document. The boundary of the toner's region is a "free boundary." The electric potential satisfies one partial differential equation outside the toner and another partial differential equation inside the toner. The potential is continuous with its first derivative across the free boundary, and its normal derivative vanishes on the free boundary. The mathematical problem represents an entirely new kind of free-boundary problem. An IMA team has shown that for some range of parameters, the problem has a unique solution and for another range of parameters, it has an infinite number of solutions. There are still many open questions regarding this problem. However, already at this stage certain important constants have been computed that may help the designer to improve the image of the photocopy.

3. Growth of crystals in solution. A large number of crystals lie in a solution within a photographic film. To achieve the best size distribution for a specific function of the film, one has to study the evolution of the crystals in time. This problem can be viewed as a dynamical system that approximates a conservation law with nonlinear nonlocal terms. The problem was considered by people at the IMA. Their analysis discovered the asymptotic size of the crystal grains; it also explained in what sense the dynamical system is a good approximation to the conservation law. So far only the case of crystals that are cube-like bodies has been considered. The next step will be to study a more realistic model where the crystals are cylinder-like.

Industrial mathematics conferences have been organized annually at the Rensselaer Polytechnic Institute. These conferences have an unusual format. The speaker, an industrial participant, presents a problem, and the conference participants, who are selected or self-selected for their interest in such events, attempt to figure out how to model the problem. They try to determine the basic variables and equations, the essential features of the problem, and the acceptable approximations. They discuss how to describe the problem through mathematical formulas. If this stage is successful, then discussion might continue on methods for the solution of the model equations. Several such problems will be considered in the course of the conference. A similar industrial clinic is organized at the Claremont Colleges; an instructor and a team of students spend typically one year working on a specific problem.

The Center for Quality and Productivity Improvement is an interdisciplinary center located at the University of Wisconsin. The staff of the center is evenly divided between statisticians and engineers. The center supports a large range of technology transfer activities, from conferences to guest lectures to consulting, and conducts a research program in quality and productivity improvement on which the technology transfer is based.

A consortium of industrial sponsors has been organized by the Institute for Oil Recovery and the Department of Mathematics at the University of Wyoming. The scientific program of the institute follows the research interests of its faculty in petroleum reservoir modeling and numerical simulation. Computational ideas and algorithms developed within the research programs of the institute are available to the industrial sponsors, including dynamically adaptive grids and characteristic methods of differencing.

At Duke University, a program was initiated in the modeling of granular flow. This problem had not been attempted previously by the mathematical community and looked rather disordered at the outset. Design engineers for grain silos had encountered various problems important to the design process that they did not understand. After some effort, it was discovered that the mathematical problems were quite interesting and were illustrative of the class of problems that change type from elliptic to hyperbolic. The change of type was associated with the formation of shear bands in the granular material, which was just the problem that had puzzled the design engineers.

A number of large industrial laboratories maintain in-house mathematics groups. These groups have similar technology transfer problems and usually succeed by taking the responsibility upon themselves for the transfer of technology. Similarly, the national laboratories have developed algorithmic, computational, and software capabilities and technology, which have been transferred to U.S. industries. A very effective method of technology transfer is to educate students who will later find employment in industrial or national laboratories. Meetings of the mathematical sciences professional societies provide a forum for technology transfer, and in some cases attract engineers and mathematical scientists from industry.

Because of the central role of computing, software is an increasingly important mechanism for technology transfer. Well-designed software allows immediate application of new advanced algorithms and techniques in disparate fields. A common route for technology transfer involves implementation of a high-level computational algorithm in a computer code. Mathematica and Nastran provide examples. Argonne National Laboratory has pioneered with the establishment of a software library, Netlib, for the electronic exchange of software. It is known for its excellent quality, and a number of its offerings, such as LINPAK, are widely used.

Often, research groups in industry pick up on academic research codes and incorporate the ideas into their in-house production and simulation codes. The scientific computing language C++ began around 1980 as a research project at AT&T Bell Laboratories. A portable translator was distributed within the Bell Laboratories and to universities for a nominal cost, thereby encouraging experimentation by users and feedback to the designer. Today the estimated number of C++ users is 100,000. Similarly the statistical language S has grown from a research tool to a commercial product that is today the de facto standard among statisticians for both research and student training. Within AT&T, S has served as the medium for moving statistical methods from the research area into development, marketing, and manufacturing.

These examples show that it is possible for technology transfer to succeed. There are a variety of ways to transfer technology. Technology users can be canvassed, to determine their needs and interests; the problem can be selected in an area where users are known to be interested; and novel areas can be found, for which users and their problem must be identified. To ensure that technology transfer occurs, the mathematical scientists, engineers, manufacturers, and business leaders must accept the task to be accomplished and plan for the result.

4.2   Simulation and Computational Modeling

Mathematical and computational analysis is an essential tool in product design and system development. Oil exploration, automotive engine design, wing and fuselage design for aircraft, circuitry components for computers, finance, robotic control, the design of novel composite materials, and construction design provide only a few examples of this fact.

- Simulating the behavior and performance of equipment or systems on a computer enables the determination of the design parameters that will significantly improve performance, or even determine whether the "thing" will work. Simulation provides such information more quickly and cheaply than the classic construction and experimentation still commonplace in many industries.

One example is the megabit memory chip that was designed and tested in nine months at AT&T Bell Laboratories. Similar design speeds have been obtained by other manufacturers. Another example is the positioning of the engine nacelle on the Boeing 737 to increase lift significantly. The manufacturer of the 737 was able to obtain substantial improvements in performance while reducing the number of wind tunnel tests from more than 60 to about 10. Highly efficient methods of computational fluid dynamics lead to airplane geometries with optimal flight characteristics and lower fuel consumption (see Figure 4.1).

Complex processes are characterized by their many interacting subprocesses. They must be efficiently designed, built, modified, and maintained with sufficient flexibility to be viable in new, flexible manufacturing environments. These goals cannot be achieved without detailed analysis and simulation of the entire system to indicate sensitivities of process output to changes in interacting component subsystems.

Although engineering and scientific computing have become central tools of engineers and scientists over the past decades, there is a potential among U.S. industries for greatly increased utilization of

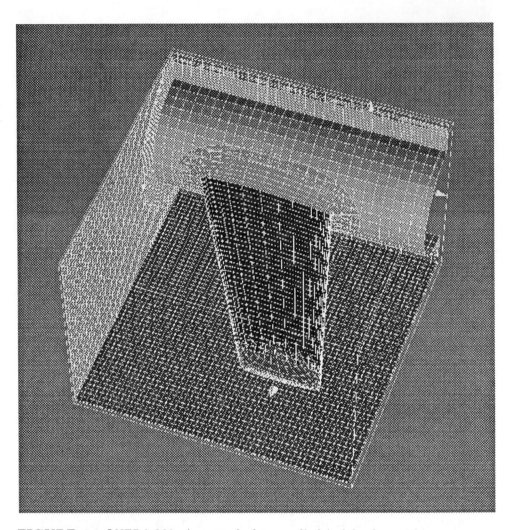

FIGURE 4.1 ONERA M6 wing attached to a cylindrical fuselage. This composite overlapping grid was generated using the program CMPGRD. These composite overlapping grids are used in modeling fluid flow around objects with complex geometrical structure. Some of their advantages over other methods are their smoothness and their ability to provide high resolution where it is needed, both of which are important for accurate modeling. The composite grid shown in this figure is used for modeling air flow around a wing. Reprinted, by permisssion, from [16]. Copyright ©1990 by Academic Press, Inc.

computers to reduce laboratory experimentation and testing (e.g., in pharmacology, design of materials, process design, and analysis of the total aerodynamical system of an aircraft).

The importance of scientific and engineering computing has been confirmed by numerous U.S. government-sponsored studies. The *Critical Technologies Plan* (see Appendix A.4) mandated by Congress identified 20 critical technologies, including the following five:

- Simulation and modeling

- Software producibility

- Parallel computer architectures

- Computational fluid dynamics

- Semiconductor devices and microelectronic circuits

Simulation and modeling have a critical role among the remaining fifteen identified technologies. Simulation has been at the heart of progress in technology and science for many reasons, including the following:

- Necessity. The cutting-edge problems that challenge engineers and scientists typically cannot be solved by other methods.

- Availability. Raw computing power is enormous and increasing rapidly.

- Feasibility. During the past several decades, there have been substantial advances in the mathematical methods and algorithmic development that unite science and technology with the computer.

Examples

Simulation technology has enriched the knowledge base and benefited the intuitive problem-solving approach used by practicing engineers. Absent such simulation, the available tools would be rather inadequate for the type of problems that are being addressed today. Aerospace and petroleum examples were mentioned earlier.

- In the microelectronics industries, the design of new semiconductor devices and the circuitry employing them can be carried out only through simulation.

- In the pharmaceutical industry, computational methods for understanding the structure of molecules (see Figure 4.2) are becoming the standard tools. The design of new drugs is widely expected to benefit greatly from a systematic use of simulation. Quantum chemistry depends heavily on large-scale high-performance computing, including simulation. Computational modeling in quantum chemistry will provide the scientific basis for new advances in pharmacology.

- In the textile industry, the computerized layout of apparel cutting patterns to minimize waste is a problem in integer programming and optimization.

Resources

Only a decade ago, computational power was measured in megaflops (millions of floating point arithmetic operations per second). It is now measured in gigaflops (billions of floating point arithmetic operations per second) and will evolve to the multiteraflop range as powerful parallel computers come on line in the years ahead. Advances in graphics enable the user to comprehend pictorially massive amounts of data and results. Wideband networks are making supercomputing widely available to engineers and scientists at geographically remote locations. At the same time, powerful workstations provide desktop computational capability formerly available only on mainframes at a limited number of central locations.

Of equal importance to the raw computing power are advances being made in mathematical sciences, including the development of algorithms for parallel processing. In the past decade, knowledge of the behavior of the equations governing such vital areas as fluid dynamics and transport phenomena has increased dramatically. New algorithms are significantly improving the stability, accuracy, and speed of solutions of such equations.

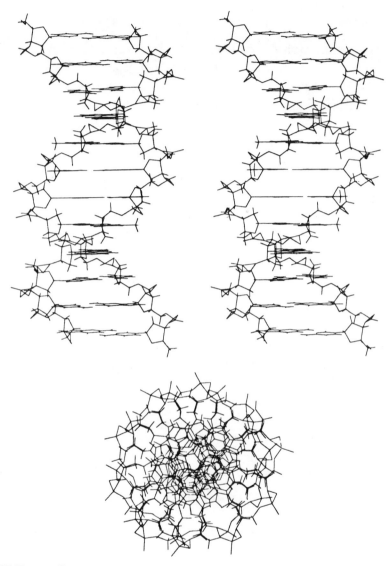

FIGURE 4.2 Computer simulation of a portion of a DNA strand, showing the three-dimensional helical form. The computation is based on the principle of minimization of an effective free energy. Computer simulation is an increasingly important method for determining the shape and structure of biological molecules and will be an increasingly powerful tool in biotechnology. Reprinted, by permission, from [13], Figure 12. Copyright ©1988 by John Wiley & Sons, Inc.

Requirements

Effective simulation depends on modeling, algorithms, and analytic understanding, as well as validation against reality. Analytic understanding is the subject of §§4.3 through 4.6. Modeling involves setting up mathematical equations whose solutions describe the behavior of the process to be modeled. The solutions must incorporate enough of the underlying science to ensure that results will be meaningful. The parameters in the equations must be observable or deducible from measurements and simple enough so their behavior can be understood. Finally, efficient and effective numerical methods for solving the equations must be developed and tested in each case.

Modeling is more than mathematical and numerical analysis—it must of necessity be an interdisciplinary effort requiring the cooperation of engineers and scientists who understand the problems and mathematicians who understand the computational and mathematical modeling process.

As technology advances and there is increased understanding, the mathematical model must be improved to represent more accurately the physical phenomena, with increases in complexity. For example, the so-called drift-diffusion equations for modeling the behavior of semiconductor devices have been very useful. However, as technology advances to the regime of submicron devices, those equations may cease to be accurate. Revision of the model to incorporate more details of the transport of electrons through a version of the Boltzmann equation or by Monte Carlo simulation is progressing. Radically new algorithms are needed at all levels to use high-performance parallel computers efficiently as well as to deal with problems of ever increasing complexity. Three-dimensional problems are orders of magnitude more complicated than two-dimensional ones. Simulation of a whole airplane is orders of magnitude more complicated than simulation of the wings. Understanding the structure and interactions of large organic molecules requires computational capability orders of magnitude larger than that required for simple molecules. System complexity will continue to increase as the underlying equations describing them incorporate more of the underlying science.

New numerical methods inherently suitable for parallel computing are needed to accommodate increasing computational demands. Such methods will need to accommodate "kernel computations," such as the solutions of systems of linear equations, the Fourier transform, and the eigenvalue and eigenvector calculations, in a structurally parallel way.

Input and output constitute another important area in which algorithmic advances are needed. The time it takes to input the geometry of the problem and generate the mesh on which many solution approaches depend is measured in weeks, whereas the time to perform the computing is measured in hours or minutes. To achieve large-scale simulation, such bottlenecks must be overcome. New methods for describing the geometry of the problem must be found. Better automatic methods to generate acceptable meshes for efficient and accurate numerical integration are urgently needed. The output of the results is equally important. Graphic representation of the results of the computations is mandatory if engineers and scientists are to make sense of them. This area of research is in its infancy, but the results are encouraging and give rise to realistic expectations that current obstacles will be overcome.

Large computer models are costly to run. The need to obtain information concerning the many parameters of the model requires efficient selection of parameter settings (inputs). This problem can be phrased as one of statistical experimental planning.

4.3   Statistical Quality Improvement

The methods and concepts of quality control and statistical design of experiments began in the 1920s. (See §4.1 for a brief history.)

Quality control began as a way to monitor or test output and thus to discard or repair defects. Statistical design of experiments in industrial contexts started as a way to identify causes of defects. The two areas have since been merged in many of their aspects. They have been transformed into a system for the building of quality into the design of products, the control of manufacturing processes to assure quality, and the installation of simple statistical tools at all stages of production to permit early detection and diagnosis of problems.

This change of emphasis was stressed by Deming in his now famous 14 points for creating quality products. Improvement is achieved by a careful study of processes and by finding and removing root causes for defects. Quality improvement is not a one-step process. It is an ongoing, incremental process. Statistical methods of experimental design are used in a trouble-shooting mode. They are not restricted to a postmanufacture testing phase, but are used by engineers, foremen, and workers on the factory floor. Those closest to the problems are directly involved in their solution.

Quality improvement results in reduced wastage, loss, and scrap and, in contrast to traditional quality control measures, is generally a cost-reducing measure. These methods are not tied to unique cultural differences between national work forces. For example, a U.S. television manufacturer was acquired by Japanese owners. The facility had a product failure rate of 146 percent, meaning that most television sets required repair, and some required multiple repairs, before manufacture was complete. After introduction of quality improvement methods, the failure rate was reduced to 2 percent, with an increase in product quality and a decrease in manufacturing costs.

Statistical methods, to be used by factory workers, must be simple and robust. The methods are not a complex set of deductive rules, but rather are a simple set of tools, to be applied experimentally to diagnose problems. Technology transfer is here a central concern. Moreover, development of appropriate statistical tools for this context is a research question currently engaging U.S. statisticians. Statistical methods for design of experiments, such as factorial designs, blocking, and randomization, are well established in agriculture but less widely used in manufacturing. The selection of significant variables from among the less important ones, the reduction in the effective dimension of large or high dimensional data sets, and response surface methods are useful in data analysis. The value of these methods is greatly enhanced when developed into convenient and robust computer software, and supported by good graphical representations.

Quality improvement in manufacturing is not the end of the story. Quality is carried upstream to the design of products and the design of the manufacturing process. Quality by design, as this is called, requires collaboration among statisticians and engineers working with design, manufacturing, and quality. An example of an issue that arises in quality by design is the reduction of the variability of certain attributes of the product, as a function of the corresponding variability of the components. The manufacturing process provides an enormous wealth of information about itself, which is normally not used in a serious way. Automated control provides a method for the use of this information in a self-learning or machine intelligence mode. Design variables for control of a chemical process (for example, temperature and pressure) might be specified initially through the solution of some model equation, which approximates the true manufacturing process. The role of automated control is to observe these control variables and ensure that they attain their desired values. However, one could also monitor the output for some measure of manufacturing quality and force the control variables to search in a small neighborhood of their specified design values for the optimum values, which give the best output.

Today, simulation models are prevalent and increasingly used to provide the data needed to achieve quality by design. Use of computer models in engineering design requires determination of many design parameters, often interacting in complicated ways. Statistical methods of experimental design; fitting of response surfaces in high dimensions, often with limited data; handling of large data sets; and statistical methods of data reduction are examples of the ideas and tools coming from statistics that will aid the design by simulation process, just as they have traditionally aided the experimental design process. What can be done for the design of products can also be transferred further "upstream" to the design of the manufacturing process.

Quality improvement is not the unique province of statistics. All the areas of the technology base (for example, simulation, modeling, and theory in engineering design) contribute to manufacturing quality.

4.4 Differential Equations

Differential equations are widely used in the modeling of natural phenomena. They are the basis of every one of the physical sciences and of the associated technology. Thus it is no surprise that they play a central role in the technology base required for economic competitiveness.

Asymptotics

Early in this century, boundary layer theory was developed as a powerful tool to attack nonlinear flow problems in a realistic way.

Asymptotic methods and singular perturbation theory provide insights into many critical phenomena in chemistry and physics, from shock waves to phase diagrams. Asymptotic theories depend on a small (or large) parameter and the possibly singular behavior that can result from small changes in a system. Usually, problems with this character are hard to handle, numerically, and special insight can be derived from analytic treatment. Stiff differential equations are one of the most successful theories of asymptotics. The equations have a very high technological significance in many areas, such as stability of chemical reactors, electrical and mechanical systems, and the design of semiconductors. Numerical algorithms, mathematical theory, and excellent software packages have been developed. Engineering-based CAD/CAM packages and computer codes depend on numerical algorithms based on the theory of stiff ordinary differential equations. Technology transfer has occurred rapidly in this area. Large systems of equations and parallel algorithms are still to be explored.

The geometric theory of diffraction is an approximation to the wave and Schrödinger equations. It has widespread application throughout physics and engineering and has been extended to apply to very general equations. Wavelets are a promising idea for the representation of solutions of differential equations. Fast potential algorithms give rapid solutions to important but special equations and are likely to become very important.

Nonlinear Phenomena

Most problems of interest and importance are nonlinear. Traveling wave pulses in fiber optics depend on nonlinearities in their governing equation to preserve their wave form. The equations come from a special class (integrable or nearly integrable equations). The theory of these equations depends on fairly esoteric mathematics, including analysis, algebra, and topology. A major breakthrough has been achieved in recent years in the development of this theory. Related equations arise in the description of water waves and other applications.

Nonlinear conservation laws are the basic equations of classical physics. They describe the interaction of nonlinear waves in a number of contexts with wide application to technology, including fluid dynamics, elasticity, oil reservoir flow, chemically reactive flows, and phase transitions. The theory of free boundary problems describes a quite similar set of phenomena, but with more emphasis on the internal structure of the nonlinear waves, which often occur in highly localized and very thin fronts. New phenomena have recently been discovered that call into question accepted ideas and lead to the modification of widely used equations. Ideas from modern differential geometry have provided a very useful reformulation of the equations of elasticity, whereas topological concepts have been instrumental in understanding the bifurcations, or changes in structure of the solutions, as parameters are varied. These developments have considerable potential for application to technology and to science.

Inverse problems have wide application in technology; they arise in the image processing of CAT scan data (see Figures 4.3 a and b), in seismology, and in nondestructive testing. It is an area to which mathematicians have contributed extensively. Similarly, image processing and pattern recognition ideas often draw from methods in differential equations.

Stochastic Phenomena

Heterogeneous, chaotic, and stochastic solutions of differential equations are among the major challenges of this subject, as well as areas of active progress. The applications of such solutions are widespread. Consider first the case of composite materials, in which the variability is deliberate and is inserted on a controlled basis. Composites form the basis for high-technology design in aircraft, automobiles, machine tools, and many other areas. A common problem is to predict the strength and material properties of a complex material, with multiple layers, holes, or constituents mixed in a coarse-grained fashion. It is also necessary to design the material, i.e., the fine-grained layering, holes, and so on, to achieve optimal material properties, such as the strength-to-weight ratio (see Figure 4.4).

More commonly, the variability is not controlled but is imposed from the outside or arises spontaneously, from instabilities in the equations. Turbulence and multiphase mixing are examples. The technological examples are widespread and include the determination of drag or flow separation over an aircraft wing, the mixing of fuel and air in a carburetor, the breakup of a jet into droplets and spray, and the

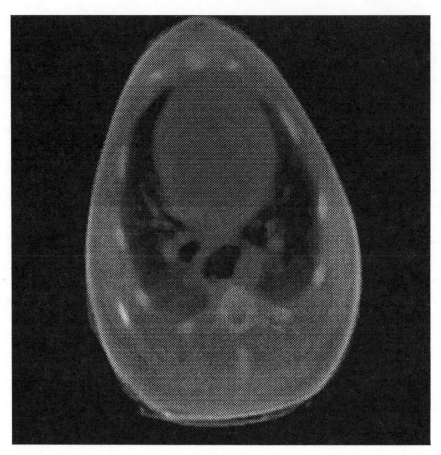

FIGURE 4.3a Improved image reconstruction methods (see Figure 4.3b) provide higher-contrast resolution of interfaces, in contrast to the resolution obtained with standard methods (Figure 4.3a). This improvement is based on new mathematical ideas and algorithms, which transform the unknown density function by a pseudodifferential operator and render the inverse problem local in terms of the tomographic data. The figures are reconstructions of the chest of a dog. The economic impact of this enhancement has been estimated at $100 million for coronary artery studies alone. Reprinted, by permission, from [14]. Copyright ©1991 by the Society for Industrial and Applied Mathematics.

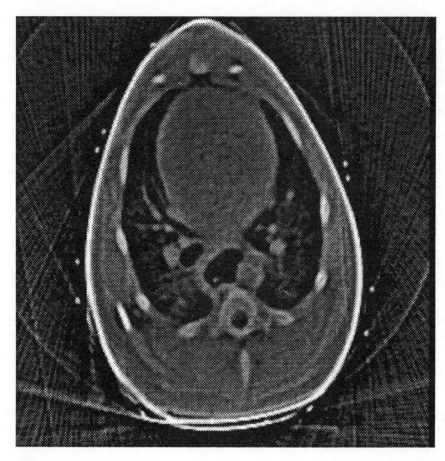

FIGURE 4.3b Improved image reconstruction methods for same image as in Figure 4.3a. Reprinted, by permission, from [14]. Copyright ©1991 by the Society for Industrial and Applied Mathematics.

mixing of the flame front in the turbulent flow in an engine cylinder. These problems are studied with a mixture of computational and statistical methods. Averaging is used to derive new equations in which the stochastic aspects have been removed and replaced by mean or effective quantities. Careful numerical and statistical studies provide a test of the validity of these averaging procedures. Interfaces between two fluids, when unstable, give rise to stochastic mixing phenomena. Frequently, this phenomenon has important economic implications, as in the solidification of alloys, where nonuniform mixing, or fingers, may degrade strength, or in oil recovery, where fingering results in poor recovery. Similar issues arise in many other technological contexts, such as the relation of material strength to microscopic descriptions involving lattice defects, voids, and microfractures and in the derivation of flow equations through porous media. To date, substantial progress has been made in the understanding of viscous flow through porous media, a necessary precondition for meaningful attempts at secondary and tertiary oil recovery. Also related are the propagation of waves in random media and localization theory, important for condensed matter physics. Mathematical scientists have been involved in the successful solution of problems in all of these areas.

Chaos theory has shown that simple-looking systems may have very complicated solutions, which appear to be stochastic in nature and may change in an irregular fashion from periodic or quasi-periodic behavior to more complex chaotic behavior in time.

Control Theory

For control theory, passive description of the solution is insufficient. Control theory has asymptotic, nonlinear, and stochastic aspects, as in the examples given above. The goal of the theory is to change (i.e., control or optimize) the solution, for example, by changing the equations or parts of the data that specify the solution. This is a common engineering problem: opening and closing valves and controlling speed or varying temperature to ensure that a process operates correctly. Control theory is thus basic to all automated manufacturing processes. Chemical plants often contain hundreds of control devices. Recently, advanced algorithms such as state estimators and multivariate controllers have been adopted. High volume and precision result

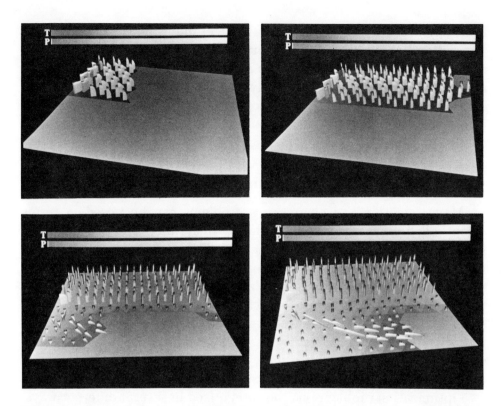

FIGURE 4.4 Visualization of plastic flow used for injection molding. The wedge-shaped glyph has a direction and length that indicate flow velocity. The velocity is confined to the horizontal plane but depends on height as well as position in the plane, which accounts for the vertical structure of the glyph. Stationary regions are indicated by a cylindrical glyph, and regions devoid of plastic have no glyph associated with them. Temperature and pressure are indicated by color shading, not shown here. Dynamics is indicated by animation. The top panel on the left shows the three basic glyphs (wedge, cylinder, and the absence of a glyph). The other three panels show single frames taken from the animation. These simulations were run on the CRAY XMP/48 supercomputer at the National Center for Supercomputing Applications at the University of Illinois at Champaign-Urbana. Reprinted, by permission, from [15]. Copyright ©1988 by the Society for Computer Simulation.

from automated hot strip mills in the steel industry. The control systems often use multilevel, multivariate adaptive control. The use of control theory and microprocessors in automobiles will increase greatly in the coming years. As a currently existing example, antilock brakes are based on feedback control. Automated control may allow operation in a regime that human control could not attain, as in the fly-by-wire control of advanced aircraft.

4.5   Optimization, Discrete, and Combinatorial Mathematics

Many scientific and engineering problems can be posed in terms of optimization, namely seeking the optimal value of some objective function by varying certain parameters. The definitions of the objective function and parameters depend on the problem. For example, the cost of a design can be minimized by an optimal selection of materials; the yield from a portfolio can be maximized by varying one's stock holdings. In most real problems, meaningful parameter values are restricted by constraints that arise from properties of the system or process to be optimized. For instance, physical laws or financial/political considerations may need to be satisfied for the solution to be feasible.

Optimization problems can be categorized in several different ways, depending on the nature of the parameters, the special forms of the objective and/or constraint functions, problem size, connections among the variables, the level and quality of information, the desired accuracy, the computing resources available, and so on. The most efficient solution methods are specialized to exploit characteristics of specific problems.

Serious use of optimization to solve practical problems began during and after World War II and was made possible by the rapid development of computer technology. A measure of the enormous progress in optimization algorithms since that time is that algorithmic improvements in many areas have matched or even exceeded gains in computing power. For example, quasi-Newton methods, developed in the 1960s, require only first-derivative information but, close to the solution, converge very rapidly, whereas the only method previously available could display arbitrarily slow convergence or fail to converge even on simple problems.

Discrete optimization is a significant new aspect of optimization that has been opened up by the advent of modern computers. Its problems involve choosing the best outcome from a huge collection of possibilities, such as the tour of service sites, which minimizes the distance traveled. These problems are extremely difficult to solve, because there is no global analysis or local measure, such as a gradient, to guide the convergence toward an optimal solution. Optimization problems arise in many practical situations, such as motion planning for a robotic machine tool.

Sequential Quadratic Programming Methods

Enormous progress has been made within the past 15 years in the development of algorithms for solving optimization problems that include nonlinear constraints. A great step forward has been the development of sequential quadratic programming (SQP) methods, which solve a sequence of simplified subproblems containing linearizations of the nonlinear constraints. SQP methods have been remarkably successful in solving problems that were considered intractable in the 1970s. Their success in solving well-known test problems led to the creation of reliable implementations in general-purpose software. The success of these codes then led to the development of SQP methods specialized for particular problems.

For example, in the 1980s the Electric Power Research Institute (EPRI) commissioned a project to apply state-of-the-art optimization methods to solve the important and troublesome optimal power flow (OPF) problem. The OPF problem has many forms, all of which involve minimizing a nonlinear function (say, the cost of maintaining and operating an electrical network), subject to nonlinear constraints representing the power flow equations as well as physical limitations on the system. The "folklore" prior to the 1980s was that OPF problems were "bumpy," i.e., had numerous local optima, and hence it was believed that problems of realistic size were extremely difficult, if not impossible, to solve. The "happy ending" is that these difficulties were shown to arise from inadequate numerical optimization methods rather than being inherent to the OPF problem. In fact, when a general-purpose SQP method was applied, the solutions were found to be well behaved and could be computed efficiently and reliably.

Based on this initial success, General Electric and other companies that produce power network management systems now market software packages that apply specialized SQP methods to the OPF problem. Because large power systems are enormously expensive to operate and contain many fixed costs that cannot be lowered, any improvement in efficiency has a significant financial effect. For example, one power company reduced the power loss in its system by 3 percent per year, leading to an estimated annual savings of $2.5 million.

The scenario just described for the OPF problem illustrates a frequent pattern in the successful application of mathematical sciences: once a previously intractable problem has been solved, expectations rise accordingly.

Real-world optimization problems almost never arise in isolation, to be solved once and then to disappear. Rather, success with one problem leads its formulators to seek to solve larger and more complicated problems in the same vein or in closely related areas. In the case of the OPF, power engineers now want to solve ever-larger problems, to carry out operational planning under various contingencies, and to reoptimize the network in real time when changes in the system occur, such as weather-related damage to the power system.

Linear Programming

An area of great excitement in optimization since 1984 has been the development of interior methods to solve very large linear programming (LP) problems. Linear programming is a fundamental building block for most branches of optimization. It has a broad range of applications, for example, oil refinery planning, airline crew scheduling, and telephone routing. For nearly 40 years, the only practical method for solving these problems was the simplex method, which has been very successful for moderate-sized problems, but is incapable of handling very large problems.

Interior methods rely on more general nonlinear transformations and work efficiently on some large structured linear programs with which the simplex method has difficulty. Using interior methods, AT&T has been able to solve planning and routing problems that were previously unsolvable because of size—for example, long-range facility planning in the Pacific basin.

The development of interior methods has led to remarkable advances in the simplex algorithm. New implementations are competitive with interior-based methods on many problems, and either method can prove to be superior. This is an example of how results in one area of mathematics can encourage development in other areas. The net result is that large, important problems can now be solved.

Discrete Optimization

Applications of discrete optimization are revolutionizing the way products are manufactured, ordered, stored, and delivered. With proper mathematical scheduling techniques, one has prompt fulfillment of orders, with striking economic consequences. Until a few years ago, almost all shoes sold in this country were manufactured abroad. This is no longer the case, thanks to efficient computerized techniques for restocking inventories in a rapid and competitive way. These inventory methods have shifted the competitive balance in favor of domestic industry.

Efficient scheduling and routing of expensive human resources and equipment are allowing the private and public sectors to do more with less. With combinatorial optimization techniques, New York City reworked sanitation crew schedules to save $25 million a year with better service and more convenient work schedules. U.S. airlines need fewer planes and personnel to cover the same number of weekly flights and are better able to respond to weather disruptions through the use of advanced combinatorial algorithms for scheduling. The American Airlines computer-based reservation and scheduling scheme and the algorithms on which it is based are credited in the press as being a significant contributor to that carrier's competitive success. American Airlines, in cooperation with IBM, designed a mixed integer crew scheduling model at a scale that would have been unsolvable three years ago.

IBM's European manufacturing plants all have groups or access to groups that have been users of IBM's mathematical programming products for years. An example of the type of problem solved is the "implosion" problem providing a list of parts needed at various times in order to meet a production schedule. Availability of parts from various vendors may be part of the problem. Another type of problem, solved at GM for example, is a production allocation-distribution problem with allowances for changeovers, overtime, and layoffs at plants. At one plant they reported that the use of this model saved more than $1 per car, which amounted to a considerable level of savings.

For the Weyerhaeuser Company, one of the largest forest products companies in the world, profit levels depend considerably on how trees are cut up into logs and how the resulting logs are allocated to different markets. These decisions about how to use raw materials are made by workers in the field, operating at high speed. The revenue Weyerhaeuser derives from any particular log depends on many factors: length, diameter, curvature, and knot and quality characteristics.

A decision simulator was developed to implement dynamic programming-based improvements in Weyerhaeuser's raw materials returns. The simulator provides the user with a way to cut and allocate tree stems, receive immediate feedback on the economic consequences of the decisions, and see for comparison the dynamic programming decisions and their economic consequences. Workers on site in forests and at mills quickly became comfortable with the system. Using the simulator, they continually improve their own decision-making capabilities. Operational benefits of the system have exceeded $100 million in increased profits.

Combinatorial optimization is a central methodology in theoretical computer science and in most large software systems. Although other countries equal or lead the United States in many aspects of computer memory and processor design, the United States still has a large lead in software and the underlying theory. In the last year, some Japanese computer firms established research centers in theoretical computer science in the United States, staffed by Americans.

Algebraic Methods

A major feature of twentieth-century technology has been the development and exploitation of new communications media. Mathematical laws governing the capacity of systems to transmit, store, and process information are the subject of information theory. Redundant signaling is necessary for reliable transmission, and coding theory is concerned with constructive methods of introducing redundancy—for example, the addition of a parity check to a binary word to detect a single bit error. Error-detecting and error-correcting codes are an integral and essential part not only of the modern telecommunications industry, but also of every industry in which information is stored, retrieved, and transmitted. A scratched compact disc continues to "play true" because of an error-correcting code, which occurs similarly for disc drives, magnetic tapes, and all forms of stored and communicated data. The use of symbolic dynamics has allowed more efficient storage of data on discs, with perhaps a 5 percent improvement in a product with a $10 million annual market. The demand for protection of privacy and provision of electronic signatures generated by the spread of electronic communication networks has stimulated extensive research in cryptology. Cryptographic methods are already widely used for protection of automatic teller machine communications and for pay-TV access control. Very soon they will be used for protection of electronic mail and transmissions from portable telephones. Recent research has been extremely successful in developing fundamental new ideas, such as that of public-key cryptography, as well as in designing practical systems. Further work is necessary to find faster and even simpler systems that are still secure, since the schemes known at present often require excessive amounts of computing power.

4.6 Statistical and Probabilistic Models

Stochastic Modeling

Stochastic modeling is the study of phenomena in which "uncertainty" is caused by the inconsistency of natural phenomena or by sources that elude control. The uncertainty in stochastic models is recognized and included directly in the model as input, instead of the model being treated deterministically. Stochastic modeling areas such as simulation, queuing theory, dynamic programming, statistical quality control, and reliability have already been alluded to. These techniques have become an essential tool in business, government, and industry.

In a systematic effort to reduce inventories and manage assets, EPRI developed an industry-wide utility fuel inventory model using stochastic modeling. The task involved uncertainties due to supply disruptions and demand fluctuations. The inventory model balances a utility's customer service goals against these risks. The model is based on risk analysis, dynamic programming, and simulation, and enables a utility to evaluate an array of fuel management policies in order to meet service goals in a cost-effective manner. This inventory model has been used by 79 utilities to realize annual savings of over $125 million.

An example of the use of stochastic modeling outside of the manufacturing context is given in a report of the President's Commission on Aviation Safety [17], issued in April 1988, on the strengths, weaknesses, and problems of the airspace system together with 15 recommendations for change. One of these recommendations stated that "Operations research [applied mathematics methods and models for solving complex optimization problems] should be recognized as a standard approach for problem solving in the FAA." As an example, when the safety of navigation standards over the North Atlantic was questioned by the International Federation of Airline Pilots Association in the 1960s, an operations research study, which included the assessment of collision risk, resulted in a resolution that both minimized cost and maximized safety.

Decision analysis was used to evaluate and select emission control equipment for three units of Ohio Edison's W. H. Sammis coal-fired power plant. With this technique, electrostatic precipitators were chosen over fabric filters, resulting in a savings of approximately $1 million. The modeling of the Long Island blood distribution system as an inventory problem, using Markov chains, and its optimal solution resulted in a reduction of wastage by 80 percent, which has translated into an annual savings of $500,000. Delivery costs were reduced by 64 percent, which has meant an annual savings of $100,000. Decision analysis, reliability theory, and Markov processes were used to plan and design the water supply system of the Palo Verde Nuclear Generating Station near Phoenix. A cost savings of approximately $20 million was achieved, and the reliability of an innovative water supply system was assured.

Spatial Statistics

Statistical variability can arise in observed data associated with locations in space, so that the random variable $\xi = \xi(\vec{x})$ is a function of the spatial coordinate $\vec{x}$. Such is the case with geostatistics, of importance to petroleum reservoir modeling and mining. The statistically most probable values of ξ, given partial geological data, are constructed by kriging, which is a variance minimization algorithm. Further, representative variability can be added by the use of random fields, conditioned on the known data.

Agricultural field experiments depend on statistics for the analysis of data. The goal of these experiments is to compare different varieties of the same crop or different schedules for the application of fertilizer, water, and so on. Since the test plot will typically not be uniform with respect to other variables, such as sunlight or fertility, careful statistical design of the experiment and statistical analysis of the data are required. These are ongoing areas of statistical research, to which significant efforts are devoted. They have been highly successful and have been important contributors to the strong position in agricultural technology enjoyed by the United States.

Image enhancement and computer vision make use of random fields and spatial statistics. Commercial application of this technology includes biomedical devices, such as the CAT scan and automated medical diagnosis, and industrial devices, such as the design of intelligent robots and the use of ultrasound to test for defects in metal welds or pipe castings.

4.7 Manpower, Education, and Training

The mathematical sciences community has the primary responsibility for the collegiate mathematics education of engineers and scientists. It has provided significant portions of the intellectual leadership in efforts to revitalize education at the K-12 levels and has sole responsibility for graduate- and professional-level education in the mathematical sciences. Just at a time when increased use of mathematics across many disciplines has raised the requirements for mathematical reasoning on the part of students, there have been ongoing problems with the motivation of U.S. students to learn mathematics. These two events have prompted serious and high-level examination of the entire educational aspect of the mathematical sciences.

A major increase in instruction in necessary mathematical methods is occurring in contemporary higher education in the natural and social sciences, engineering, and business. For majors in the mathematical sciences, the departmental lines are disappearing. A recent survey of American universities showed that the enrollments in advanced mathematics courses taught outside the mathematical sciences departments exceed similar enrollments within those departments. In addition, the majority of those with a B.S. degree in mathematics who subsequently obtain a Ph.D. earn it in a field outside of mathematics. As one striking example of the blurring of departmental lines, more computer science faculty have Ph.D.s in mathematics than in computer science. This growth in the use of mathematics has occurred at more than the advanced level. Indeed, what was once considered advanced mathematical training is now becoming essential knowledge for many future blue-collar jobs. In Japan, working on an automobile assembly line requires that employees with only a high school diploma perform statistical quality control calculations.

American higher education has an unsurpassed reputation for producing creative researchers. The relatively few college students requiring very advanced mathematical training have been especially successfully educated. But the future challenge posed by large numbers of students in college (and, more importantly, in high school) needing much more mathematical training is made more difficult by the common U.S. assumption that most students lack the motivation to learn mathematics. Already the pipeline of students in mathematically oriented disciplines who are U.S. citizens or permanent residents is running low. Half or more of the Ph.D.s in mathematics and many engineering disciplines are being awarded to foreign nationals.

Heartening examples prove that students can be motivated to do much better: Jaime Escalante's Garfield High School students, publicized in the movie *Stand and Deliver*, and the mathematics majors of SUNY College at Potsdam, who number 20 percent of that college's baccalaureates (nationally, math majors account for about 1 percent of college graduates). The achievement of Escalante was given independent confirmation through U. Treisman's success at the University of California, Berkeley, with minority students taking calculus. Translating a few bright spots into a national agenda for excellence in mathematics education is the announced goal of the Mathematical Sciences Education Board of the National Research Council and of the joint Education Conference of the President and Governors. The importance of this mission cannot be overstated.

Besides the problem of improving students' motivation to learn mathematics, there are difficult questions about how to teach mathematics. It is a challenge to find appropriate underlying themes on which to organize the teaching of mathematics more efficiently. There is already much more mathematics that busy students in the sciences should know than will fit into their schedules. In primary and secondary school, mathematics follows a relatively sequential program of integer addition to integer multiplication to fraction arithmetic to algebra to analytic geometry to calculus. But probability and statistics, matrix algebra, and computer-oriented discrete mathematics topics and diverse applications also demand attention. At the college level, the trail branches out in many directions. Efforts of the "New Math" in the 1960s to modernize school mathematics were largely a failure, although many of the country's best mathematical minds were involved. Unfortunately this failure halted for many years any further attempt to make the major changes required in mathematical education. Recent efforts such as the National Conference of Teachers of Mathematics (NCTM) standards [18] and the National Science Foundation/Mathematical Association of America Calculus Reform project show that mathematicians are now attacking these difficult educational issues once more.

There is currently substantial debate within collegiate mathematics departments concerning the required content of a major in mathematics. So many facets of both pure and applied mathematics exist that a consensus on what constitutes the central core of training in mathematics has yet to emerge. The explosion of new fields and new uses of mathematics continues to present serious educational challenges that must be addressed.

Because the mathematical sciences community has only recently returned to these educational issues in a serious way, because of the great importance of science and technical education to economic competitiveness and other important national issues, and because of the sizable fraction that mathematics occupies within science and technical education as a whole, there is a strong need for the mathematical sciences community to recognize the seriousness of the issues described in this report and to assume responsibility for further action.

5 FINDINGS AND RECOMMENDATIONS

Findings

The principal finding of this report is as follows:

- **The mathematical sciences are vital to economic competitiveness. They are a critical, generic, enabling technology.**

Six points complement and elaborate on this finding.

- Applications of the mathematical sciences arise in all aspects of the product cycle and across the technology base.

- Applications also arise from highly diverse areas of the mathematical sciences; they depend on the vitality of research in the mathematical sciences and draw on this research as a technology base.

- Computation and modeling recur as central themes. They are a primary route for technology transfer from the mathematical sciences.

- Technology transfer, from the research to the industrial sector, is of critical importance for the enhancement of economic competitiveness.

- In the mathematical sciences (as elsewhere), technology transfer occurs seriously below its potential. The transfer of technology will be accomplished best if the creators of technology assume the primary responsibility for its transfer. Also helpful is an atmosphere of cooperation among the industrial, governmental, and academic sectors, an atmosphere in which the central importance of technology transfer is clearly understood by the participants in the process.

- Technology transfer, computational and mathematical modeling, and education have an importance to economic competitiveness that is very large relative to the recognition given to these activities by the academic mathematical sciences community.

- Manpower and technical training are also crucial for economic competitiveness. The mathematical sciences community has a significant responsibility in this area.

The ability of the mathematical sciences community to deliver short-term results with any degree of consistency depends crucially on healthy support for its long-term development. Conversely, the more fundamental areas of the mathematical sciences are continually invigorated by interaction with applications. It is an almost universal experience that once an application succeeds, further progress depends on the development of new, and often fundamental, theories. The Board on Mathematical Sciences endorses the principle that short-term applications and fundamental theories are virtually inseparable. Detailed studies of the health and vitality of the mathematical sciences technology base have been conducted (see, e.g., [19] and [20]). Their primary conclusion was that renewal of the U.S. mathematical sciences was at risk owing to weaknesses in manpower and training, and to a lack of balance in the funding level for the mathematical sciences. Widespread underinvestment in the mathematical sciences was documented in these reports. The recommendations were to increase the priority given to manpower and training and to eliminate the funding deficiencies.

- The board endorses the conclusions and recommendations of the reports *Renewing U.S. Mathematics: Critical Resource for the Future* [19] and *Renewing U.S. Mathematics: A Plan for the 1990s* [20], to assure future manpower availability, correct funding imbalances, and preserve the vitality of fundamental research in the mathematical sciences.

Engineering and manufacturing research and design depend heavily on computational and mathematical modeling. Both the knowledge base and the problem-solving approach of the practicing engineer have benefited increasingly from simulation and, absent such simulation, would be totally inadequate for the types of problems that are being addressed today. Increased involvement of the mathematical sciences community in all aspects of production research is a low-cost, highly effective means of improving and accelerating production. Computational and mathematical modeling have been emphasized in many studies, leading to a major policy statement by the U.S. government [21].

- The board endorses the conclusions and recommendations of *The Federal High Performance Computing Program* [21].

The mathematical sciences community has the primary responsibility for collegiate mathematics education of engineers and scientists. They have provided significant portions of the intellectual leadership in efforts to revitalize education at the K-12 levels. They have sole responsibility for graduate- and professional-level education in the mathematical sciences. Just at a time when increased use of mathematics across many disciplines has raised the requirements for mathematical reasoning on the part of students, there have been ongoing problems with U.S. students being motivated to learn mathematics. These two events have prompted serious and high-level examination of the entire educational aspect of the mathematical sciences.

- The board endorses the recommendations and conclusions of the MS 2000 project,[4] in support of education and training in the mathematical sciences. More attention must be given to the challenge of motivating students to study mathematics.

---

[4]MS 2000 is the shorthand reference to the Committee on the Mathematical Sciences in the Year 2000, a joint project of the Mathematical Sciences Education Board and the Board on Mathematical Sciences, National Research Council. See reports numbered (1), (2), and (12) in Appendix B.

Recommendations

This report makes two primary recommendations:

- **The board recommends that the mathematical sciences community significantly increase its role in the transfer of mathematical sciences technology.**

- **The board calls on the mathematical sciences community to put far greater emphasis on and give greater career recognition to activities connected with computational and mathematical modeling, technology transfer, and education.**

The mathematical sciences can be viewed as a vital technology base for the economic process. Following from this point of view, the transfer of technology is the delivery of the product. The time for technology transfer is a lengthy process; commonly accepted are estimates that it takes on the order of one or more decades for fundamental discoveries to enter into commercial use or defense applications. In the critically important case of statistical quality control and quality improvement, the time for transfer of methods of statistical experimental design to industrial use has exceeded 70 years and is still far from complete. To ensure that technology transfer occurs, mathematical scientists, engineers, manufacturers, and business leaders must accept the task to be accomplished and plan for the result. Some successful examples of such systematic and planned efforts are documented in this report (see, e.g., §§3.7, 3.9, and 4.3).

Computational and mathematical modeling, technology transfer, and education have a critical and direct connection to economic competitiveness, a connection that should be reflected in the recognition given these activities by the mathematical sciences community. Specific actions, endorsed by this report, for carrying out its two primary recommendations include the following:

- Federal and state agencies should ensure that investments in research to improve productivity include the necessary involvement and support of the mathematical sciences.

- Programs in industrial mathematics, jointly supported by industry and government, should be established in our colleges and universities and should include grants for small science and for individual investigators.

The economic competitiveness of the United States can be substantially improved by increased involvement of the mathematical sciences community. Numerous agencies currently sponsor programs that have successfully encouraged interaction between academic and government laboratory researchers. This report proposes a similar effort to stimulate increased interaction between universities and industry.

The large federally funded science and technology centers already have a mandate for technology transfer. However, many industrial problems in mathematics are of moderate size, appropriate for small science and individual investigators. Thus the board recommends a program in industrial mathematics that includes small science and individual investigators, with the goal of furthering economic competitiveness through increased contributions by mathematical scientists. By uniting existing fragmented efforts, such a program would establish industrial mathematics as a subfield of the mathematical sciences. By expanding these efforts, this program would focus the creative energies of the mathematical sciences on the vital national goal of economic competitiveness.

The mathematical sciences should also take full advantage of existing programs. Many states have industrial development programs that have paid favorable attention to well-conceived initiatives for technology transfer from the mathematical sciences. Similarly, the federal government, in addition to sponsoring programs that support a base technology, sponsors research programs oriented to the solution of problems. The mathematical sciences community should compete aggressively in such programs.

- The board urges that strong and meaningful consideration for hiring, retention, promotion, and tenure be given for achievements in research and education supporting industrial mathematics. The emphasis given to computational mathematics, modeling, and applications should be in balance with that accorded to other areas of mathematics.

- The board calls on university administrators to encourage adoption by their mathematical sciences units of criteria and procedures that promote strengthening of the ties between universities and industry.

Our national requirements for the creation of new mathematical sciences technology, as well as for effective access to this technology, call for a balance between theory and applications. Applications should be judged not only on the basis of their relation to theory, but also for their success in solving problems important to modern industrial practice, among other societal goals. Important new mathematics and entire new areas of mathematics (mathematical programming, combinatorial optimization, queuing theory, mixed elliptic-hyperbolic partial differential equations) have been developed to solve practical problems and, in the process, to understand the mathematical structure that underlies them.

- The board recommends that industry, government, and university cooperative research and education programs be encouraged and funded.

Cooperation among industry, government, and universities benefits all three. Such cooperation can take many forms, several of which exist to some extent at the present time. A simple and widespread form of interaction is a consulting relationship between a faculty member and an industrial firm. For example, a problem that must be solved may require specialized expertise that a firm does not have and probably cannot afford to maintain in-house. Using an external consultant is very cost-effective, and he or she usually gains intellectually by being exposed to interesting problems that are then often addressed in a more general form in the individual's subsequent research. Higher levels of interaction involve support for graduate students and the development of ideas into computer algorithms and computer codes. A common outgrowth of such a relationship, when successful, is the employment of the student, after his or her graduation, by the industrial firm. At this point, an important step in completing technology transfer to the industrial sector has taken place. A well-focused program can attract the support of an industry-wide consortium. Work that appears to be applied mathematics from an academic perspective may still be viewed as rather basic by industrial managers. Industrial firms often have difficulty organizing cooperative research focused on the basic problems of their industry and may find it advantageous to participate in a consortium to accomplish this goal.

- The board recommends development of course materials to support the teaching of modeling and of industrial applications of mathematics.

These course materials could be designed as short segments for insertion into existing courses, where they would add to the range of practical illustrations available for use in the present curricula. Such material exists today and has been developed systematically by the UMAP[5] and CoMAP[6] projects. The thrust of this recommendation is that curricular reform should include the expansion, modernization, and revitalization of this material, as well as its integration into the mainstream of undergraduate education. A follow-up goal would be to develop material to support full elective courses in industrial mathematics at the advanced undergraduate and graduate levels.

The purpose of this course material would be to narrow the gap between academic mathematics and the industrial uses of mathematics. The course material should broaden students' intellectual horizons as well as their technical training. It should increase their potential usefulness in an industrial organization and should increase their ability, as future teachers of mathematics to engineers, to motivate the use of mathematics in an industrial context.

Innovations that would distinguish such course materials from the usual offerings would be modeling, case studies, and industrial examples. Modeling is the process of converting a real-world problem into a mathematical problem. The end result is a mathematical formulation of the problem, for example, an equation to be solved. In problem solving, modeling is often the most important step. Case studies drawn from industrial practice would show how theory is used in practice and

---

[5]UMAP, the Undergraduate Mathematics and Its Applications Program, has been funded by the National Science Foundation. This CoMAP program produced more than 300 teaching modules and numerous monographs in the period between 1976 and 1981.

[6]CoMAP is the acronym for Consortium for Mathematics and Its Applications. Its purpose is to produce teaching modules in applied mathematics for all media. Address: 60 Lowell Street, Arlington, MA 02147.

would emphasize a problem-solving rather than a deductive approach. Each case study would be relatively short and self-contained. In this way the breadth of applicability of mathematics and the value of the other material in students' courses could be illustrated.

An excellent way to start the teaching of modeling and industrial mathematics would be to hold summer schools for advanced graduate students and junior faculty, similar to the summer schools available in theoretical physics.

- The board urges the mathematical sciences professional societies to promote intellectual activity in problem solving and modeling to strengthen the industrial use of mathematics.

Technology transfer can occur only with the full support of the people who are actively engaged in the process. The board proposes that the mathematical professional societies include technology transfer within their mission and encourage, through workshops, minisymposia, and plenary lectures, more interaction among mathematicians in industry, universities, and government laboratories. Special conferences on theoretical areas of mathematics could include the industrial perspective as well. Mathematicians in industry should be encouraged to serve in larger numbers on the editorial boards of professional journals. There is evidence that these activities are actually occurring, but the mathematical sciences community needs to pay far more attention to these issues.

REFERENCES

[1] *Economic Report of the President: Annual Report of the Council of Economic Advisors.* U.S. Government Printing Office, January 1989, p. 320.

[2] Peter Passel. "Adding up the World Trade Talks: Fail Now, Pay Later," *New York Times*, Section 4, December 16, 1990.

[3] Edmund Faltermayer. "Is 'Made in the U.S.A' Fading Away?," *Fortune*, 122, No. 7, September 24, 1990, pp. 62-73.

[4] Michael L. Dertouzos, Richard K. Lester, Robert M. Solow, and the MIT Commission on Industrial Productivity. *Made in America: Regaining the Productive Edge.* Massachusetts Institute of Technology, Cambridge, Mass., 1989.

[5] James Brian Quinn. "Technology in Services: Past Myths and Future Challenges," in *Technology in Services*, Bruce R. Guile and James Brian Quinn, eds. National Academy of Engineering, National Academy Press, Washington, D.C., 1988.

[6] *A Strategic Industry at Risk.* A Report to the President and the Congress from the National Advisory Committee on Semiconductors. Ian M. Ross, chairman, November 1989.

[7] Wenjie Dong, Mark Jeffrey Emanuel, Phillip Bording, and Norman Bleistein. *A Computer Implementation of 2.5D Common Shot Inversion.* Report CWP-090P. Center for Wave Phenomena, Department of Mathematical and Computer Sciences, Colorado School of Mines, Golden, Colo., October 1990.

[8] "A New Era for Auto Quality," *Business Week*, October 22, 1990, pp. 84-96.

[9] *The Technological Dimensions of International Competitiveness.* A Report to the Council of the National Academy of Engineering. Committee on Technology Issues That Impact International Competitiveness. Washington, D.C., 1988, pp. 23 ff.

[10] Judy P. Lewent. "The Finances of Doing Something About Health," *MIT Management*, Fall 1988, pp. 20-24.

[11] Amal Kumar Naj. "In R & D, the Next Best Thing to a Gut Feeling," *Wall Street Journal*, May 21, 1990, p. A9.

[12] S. Myers. "The New Look of Capital Spending," *Fortune*, March 13, 1989, pp. 115-120.

[13] Tamar Schlick. "A Modular Strategy for Generating Starting Conformations and Data Structures for Polynucleotide Helices for Potential Energy Calculations," *Journal of Computational Chemistry*, 9, 1988, 861-889.

[14] Adel Faridani, Erik L. Ritman, and Kennan T. Smith. "Local Tomography," *SIAM Journal of Applied Mathematics*, 1991, in press.

[15] R. Ellson and D. Cox. "Visualization of Injection Molding," *Simulation*, 51, No. 5, 184-188, November 1988.

[16] G. Chesshire and W. D. Henshaw. "Composite Overlapping Meshes for the Solution of Partial Differential Equations," *Journal of Computational Physics*, 90, 1-64, September 1990.

[17] *Aviation Safety Commission.* Final Report and Recommendations, Vol. 1. The White House, Washington, D.C., April 1988.

[18] *Curriculum and Evaluation Standards for School Mathematics.* National Council of Teachers of Mathematics, Reston, Va., March 1989.

[19] *Renewing U.S. Mathematics: Critical Resource for the Future.* Ad Hoc Committee on Resources for the Mathematical Sciences. National Academy Press, Washington, D.C., 1984.

[20] *Renewing U.S. Mathematics: A Plan for the 1990s.* Committee on the Mathematical Sciences: Status and Future Directions. Board on Mathematical Sciences. National Academy Press, Washington, D.C., 1990.

[21] *The Federal High Performance Computing Program.* Office of Science and Technology Policy, The White House, Washington, D.C., September 8, 1989.

APPENDICES

Appendix A
Studies of Advanced Technology and Economic Competitiveness

Advanced technology and economic competitiveness have been the subject of a number of high-level governmental, industrial, and academic inquiries. Some of the key studies in recent years are summarized below. There is a common ground in the conclusions reached. For the purposes of this report, one should note that computations and modeling occur frequently in the conclusions of these studies and that computation and mathematical modeling are important contributors to many priority areas, even when this fact is not mentioned explicitly. In one of the studies, *The Federal High Performance Computing Program*, computational modeling is a central focus.

1. Emerging Technologies from the Department of Commerce

Twelve emerging technologies were identified by the Department of Commerce, with annual sales projected to be $350 billion by the end of the century. These technologies are as follows:

1. Advanced Materials

2. Supercomputers

3. Advanced Semiconductor Devices

4. Digital Imaging Technology

5. High-Density Data Storage

6. High-Performance Computing

7. Optoelectronics

8. Artificial Intelligence

9. Flexible Computer-Integrated Manufacturing

10. Sensor Technology

11. Biotechnology

12. Medical Devices and Diagnostics

In addition to presenting this list, the Department of Commerce report also states that at present the United States is judged to be ahead in 6 of the 12 technologies in comparison with Japan and 9 of the 12 technologies in comparison with Europe. The United States is behind in 5 areas compared with Japan and 1 compared with Europe. However, future trends are less promising. In comparison with Japan, the United States is gaining ground in none of these areas, holding even in 2, and losing ground in 10. In comparison with Europe, the United States is gaining in 3 sectors, holding even in 6, and losing in 3.

Source: *Emerging Technologies. A Survey of Technical and Economic Opportunities.* Technology Administration. U.S. Department of Commerce, Spring 1990.

2. The Federal High Performance Computing Program

The Federal High Performance Computing Program is an interagency effort led by the Office of Science and Technology Policy in response to a report issued by the Federal Coordinating Council for Science, Engineering, and Technology (FCCSET, usually referred to as "Fixit"),[7] calling for a five-year strategy for federally supported R&D in high-performance computing. High-performance computing represents a multibillion dollar world market, in which the United States is increasingly being challenged.

---

[7] *The U.S. Computer Industry.* The White House, Washington, D.C., December 1987. See also the *Annual Report FY 1989* of the FCCSET Subcommittee on Science and Engineering Computing, issued in March 1988.

Allan Bromley, in his letter of transmittal for the report, states, "We cannot afford to cede our historical leadership in high-performance computing and in its applications." From this report is reproduced a list of grand challenges, whose solution is judged to be possible, using systems developed under the initiative. At least five of these grand challenges have a direct and immediate bearing on economic compet- itiveness: material sciences, semiconductor design, design of drugs, combustion systems, and oil and gas recovery. Others of the grand challenges have a longer range or are indirectly related to this issue.

1. Prediction of Weather, Climate, and Global Change. The aim is to understand the coupled atmosphere-ocean, biosphere system in enough detail to be able to make long-range predictions about its behavior. Applications include understanding CO_2 dynamics in the atmosphere, ozone depletion, climatological perturbations owing to man-made releases of chemicals or energy into one of the component systems, and detailed predictions of conditions in support of military missions.

   Agencies: DOE, DOD, NASA, NOAA

2. Challenges in Materials Sciences. High-performance computing has provided invaluable assistance in improving our understand- ing of the atomic nature of materials. These have an enormous impact on our economy. A selected list of such materials includes semiconductors, such as silicon and gallium arsenide, and super- conductors such as the high-T_c copper oxide ceramics that have been shown recently to conduct electricity at about 100 K.

   Agencies: DOD, DOE, NSF, NASA

3. Semiconductor Design. As intrinsically faster materials such as gallium arsenide are used, a fundamental understanding is re- quired of how they operate and how to change their characteris- tics. Essential understanding of overlay formation, trapped struc- tural defects, and the effect of lattice mismatch on properties is needed. Currently, it is possible to simulate electronic proper- ties for simple regular systems; however, materials with defects and mixed atomic constituents are beyond present capabilities. Agencies: DOD, DOE, NSF

4. Superconductivity. The discovery of high-temperature superconductivity in 1986 has provided the potential of spectacular energy-efficient power transmission technologies, ultrasensitive instrumentation, and devices using phenomena unique to superconductivity. The materials supporting high-temperature superconductivity are difficult to form, stabilize, and use, and the basic properties of the superconductor must be elucidated through a vigorous fundamental research program.

Agencies: DOE, NSF, DOD

5. Structural Biology. The function of biologically important molecules can be simulated by computationally intensive Monte Carlo methods in combination with crystallographic data derived from nuclear magnetic resonance measurements. Molecular dynamics methods are required for the time-dependent behavior of such macromolecules. The determination, visualization, and analysis of these three-dimensional structures are essential to the understanding of the mechanisms of enzymic catalysis, recognition of nucleic acids by proteins, antibody/antigen binding, and many other dynamic events central to cell biology.

Agencies: DOE, HHS, NSF

6. Design of Drugs. Predictions of the folded conformation of proteins and of RNA molecules by computer simulation are rapidly becoming accepted as a useful, and sometimes primary tool in understanding the properties required in drug design.

Agencies: DOE, HHS, NSF

7. Human Genome. Comparison of normal and pathological molecular sequences is [currently] our most revealing computational method for understanding genomes and the molecular basis for disease. To benefit from the entire sequence of a single human will require capabilities for more than three billion subgenomic units, as contrasted with the 10,000 to 200,000 units of typical viruses.

Agencies: DOE, HHS, NSF

8. Quantum Chromodynamics (QCD). In high-energy theoretical physics, computer simulations of QCD are yielding first-principle calculations of the properties of strongly interacting elementary particles. New phenomena have been predicted, including the existence of a new phase of matter and the quark-gluon plasma. Properties under the conditions of the first microsecond of the big bang, and in the cores of the largest stars, have been calculated by simulation methods. Beyond the range of present experimental capabilities, computer simulations of grand unified "theories of everything" have been devised using QCD (lattice-gauge theory).

   Agencies: DOE, NSF

9. Astronomy. Data volumes generated by Very Large Array (VLA) or Very Long Baseline Array (VLBA) radio telescopes currently overwhelm the available computational resources. Greater computational power will significantly enhance their usefulness in exploring important problems in radio astronomy, resulting in better return on a major national investment.

   Agencies: NASA, NSF

10. Challenges in Transportation. In the nearer term, substantial contributions to vehicle performance can be made using more approximate physical modeling and reducing the amount of interdisciplinary coupling. Examples include modeling of fluid dynamical behavior for three-dimensional flow fields about complete aircraft geometries, flow inside engine turbomachinery, duct flow, and flow about ship hulls.

    Agencies: NASA, DOD, DOE, NSF, DOT

11. Vehicle Signature. Reduction of vehicle signature (acoustic, electromagnetic, thermal characteristics) is critical for low-detection military vehicles.

    Agencies: NASA, DOD

12. Turbulence. Turbulence in fluid flows affects the stability and control, thermal characteristics, and fuel performance of virtually all aerospace vehicles. Understanding the fundamental physics of

turbulence is requisite to reliably modeling flow turbulence for the analysis of realistic vehicle configuration.

Agencies: NASA, DOD, DOE, NSF, NOAA

13. Vehicle Dynamics. Analysis of the aeroelastic behavior of vehicles, and analysis of the stability and ride of vehicles are critical to assessments of land and air vehicle performance and life cycle.

Agencies: NASA, DOD, DOT

14. Nuclear Fusion. Development of controlled nuclear fusion requires understanding the behavior of fully ionized gasses at very high temperatures under the influence of strong magnetic fields in complex three-dimensional geometries.

Agencies: DOE, NASA, DOD

15. Efficiency of Combustion Systems. Attaining significant improvements in combustion efficiencies requires understanding the interplay between the flows of the various substances involved and the quantum chemistry that causes those substances to react. In some complicated cases, the quantum chemistry is beyond the reach of current supercomputers.

Agencies: DOE, NASA, DOD

16. Enhanced Oil and Gas Recovery. This challenge has two parts: to locate as much of the estimated 300 billion barrels of oil reserves in the United States and then to devise economic ways of extracting as much of it as possible. Thus improved seismic analysis techniques in addition to improved understanding of fluid flow through geological structures are required.

Agencies: DOE

17. Computational Ocean Sciences. The objective is to develop a predictive global ocean model incorporating temperature, chemical composition, circulation, and coupling to the atmosphere and other oceanographic features. This ocean model will be used with models of the atmosphere in the effort on global weather and have specific implications for physical oceanography as well.

Agencies: DOD, NASA, NSF, NOAA

18. Speech. Speech research is aimed at providing a communications interface with computers based on spoken language. Automatic speech understanding by computer is a large modeling and search problem in which billions of computations are required to evaluate the many possibilities for what a person might have said within a particular context.

Agencies: NASA, DOD, NSF

19. Vision. The challenge is to develop human-level visual capabilities for computers and robots. Machine vision requires image signal processing, texture and color modeling, geometric processing and reasoning, and object modeling. A component vision system will likely involve the integration of all of these processes with close coupling.

Agencies: NSF, DARPA, NASA

20. Undersea Surveillance for Anti-Submarine Warfare (ASW). The Navy faces a severe problem in maintaining a viable ASW capability in the face of quantum improvements in Soviet submarine technology, which are projected to be so substantial that evolutionary improvements in detection systems will not restore sufficient capability to counter their advantages. An attractive solution to this problem involves revolutionary improvements in long-range undersea surveillance which are possible using very high gain acoustic arrays and active acoustic sources for ASW surveillance. These methods will be computationally intensive; even taking advantage of inherent parallelism and judicious design of algorithms, computational demands for the projected post-2000 era submarine threat mandate achieving signal processing computational rates in excess of a trillion operations per second.

Agencies: DOD

Source: *The Federal High Performance Computing Program.* Office of Science and Technology Policy, The White House, September 8, 1989.

3. The National Academy of Engineering, 10 Outstanding Achievements

On the occasion of its 25th anniversary, the National Academy of Engineering (NAE) compiled a list of 10 outstanding engineering achievements that had occurred in the previous 25 years. The list was selected from 340 nominations, with the approval of the Council of the NAE. The runners-up were also remarkable, and included such achievements as the Alaskan pipeline, deep-water oil platforms, and cardiac pacemakers. The moon landing was placed first, as one of the outstanding engineering achievements of all time. The other achievements are listed below, approximately in chronological order.

With the exception of the moon landing, every topic on this list has a direct and immediate relation to economic competitiveness.

1. Moon Landing

2. Application Satellites

3. Microprocessor

4. Computer-Aided Design and Manufacturing

5. CAT Scan

6. Advanced Composite Materials

7. Jumbo Jet

8. Lasers

9. Fiber-Optic Communication

10. Genetically Engineered Products

Source: *Engineering and the Advancement of Human Welfare: 10 Outstanding Achievements 1964-1989.* National Academy of Engineering, National Academy Press, Washington, D.C., 1989.

4. The Departments of Defense and Energy, 20 Critical Technologies

According to congressional mandate, the secretaries of Defense and Energy submit an annual plan for the developing technologies considered most critical to national defense. The technologies for 1990 are listed below.

- Group A

    1. Composite Materials
    2. Computational Fluid Dynamics
    3. Data Fusion
    4. Passive Sensors
    5. Photonics
    6. Semiconductor Devices and Microelectronic Circuits
    7. Signal Processing
    8. Software Producibility

- Group B

    1. Air-Breathing Propulsion
    2. Machine Intelligence and Robotics
    3. Parallel Computer Architectures
    4. Sensitive Radars
    5. Signature Control
    6. Simulation and Modeling
    7. Weapon System Environment

- Group C

    1. Biotechnology Materials and Processing
    2. High Energy Density Materials
    3. Hypervelocity Projectiles
    4. Pulsed Power

5. Superconductivity

The priorities are indicated by groups, while the technologies are listed alphabetically within groups. The technologies in Group A are characterized as most pervasive, those in Group B as enabling, and those in Group C as emerging.

Source: *The Department of Defense Critical Technologies Plan.* The Pentagon, Washington, D.C., March 1990.

5. The Aerospace Industries Association (AIA), 10 Emerging Technologies for the 1990s

The United States exports far more in aerospace than it imports, but other nations are very quickly catching up in technology. The AIA calls for cooperation among government, industry, and academia to bring forth a national plan for key technologies. The goal is a dramatic increase in the productivity of available resources and a dramatic decrease in technology transfer time. The technologies were chosen by consensus of the aerospace industry as those needed to ensure the competitiveness of the United States into the twenty-first century. For each technology, a working group has been formed with the responsibility of drawing up a plan to achieve stated technology goals.

1. Advanced Composites

2. Very Large Integrated Circuits

3. Advanced Software

4. Air Breathing Propulsion

5. Rocket Propulsion

6. Advanced Sensors

7. Optical Information Processing

8. Artificial Intelligence

9. Ultrareliable Electronic Systems

10. Superconductivity

Source: *AIA Newsletter*, Vol. 1, No. 1, 1988, and Vol. 2, No. 7, 1989, Aerospace Industries Association, Washington, D.C.

6. The MIT Commission on Industrial Productivity

Michael L. Dertouzos, Richard K. Lester, Robert M. Solow, and the MIT Commission on Industrial Productivity. *Made in America: Regaining the Productive Edge*, Massachusetts Institute of Technology, Cambridge, Mass., 1989.

In 1986, MIT convened a commission to study declining U.S. industrial performance. The commission established eight working groups, each to assess a single industry, while a ninth group studied educational issues. The conclusions from these studies were synthesized into patterns of loss of competitiveness. The MIT commission cites six factors leading to this loss that are listed at the beginning of Chapter 2 of this report. Each pattern was explored in depth.

7. Technology Policy and Its Effect on the National Economy

Technology Policy and Its Effect on the National Economy, a report by the Technology Policy Task Force of the Committee on Science, Space and Technology of the House of Representatives, December 1988.

This wide-ranging report makes many of the points concerning technology transfer, quality, and education that are emphasized here. In particular it notes,

> Quality improvement is a critical feature in advancing the competitiveness of products manufactured in the United States. A survey of 600 U.S. business executives reveals that 89 percent of them believe that quality plays the most important role in improving the competitive position of U.S. industrial companies ... Americans seem strangely uninterested in improving the quality of their processes ... W. Edwards Deming, after years of disinterest by U.S. industry, took his message abroad and taught the Japanese how to produce goods of high quality at low cost ... Deming's 14 points on creating quality products are really directed at improving manufacturing technology.

Among Deming's 14 points is a call to use statistical methods for continuing improvement of quality and productivity. In addition, he highlights the need for vigorous education and training to keep people abreast of new technologies and elimination of dependence on mass inspection. The complete list of Deming's 14 points is given below.

1. Create consistency and continuity of purpose.

2. Refuse to allow commonly accepted levels of delay for mistakes, defective material, defective workmanship.

3. Eliminate the need for dependence upon mass inspection.

4. Reduce the number of suppliers. Buy on statistical evidence, not price.

5. Search continually for problems in the system and seek ways to improve it.

6. Institute modern ways of training, using statistics.

7. Focus supervision on helping people to do a better job. Provide the tools and techniques for people to have pride of workmanship.

8. Eliminate fear. Encourage two-way communication.

9. Break down barriers between departments. Encourage problem solving through teamwork.

10. Eliminate the use of numerical goals, slogans, and posters for the work force.

11. Use statistical methods for continuing improvement of quality and productivity and eliminate all standards prescribing numerical quotas.

12. Remove barriers to pride of workmanship.

13. Institute a vigorous program of education and training to keep people abreast of new developments in materials, methods, and technologies.

14. Clearly define management's permanent commitment to quality and productivity.

8. Governing America

Governing America: A Competitiveness Policy Agenda for the New Administration. Council on Competitiveness. Chairman, John A. Young, CEO, Hewlett-Packard, 1989.

In its recommendations, this report emphasizes technology transfer, education, and R&D. To quote, "Two priorities in science and technology stand out: facilitating the commercialization of technology and strengthening the U.S. technology infrastructure." The report recommends that the United States "Increase government investment in education, facilities and equipment that constitute the nation's technology infrastructure ... widen the focus of national research and development efforts ... promote cooperative R&D among industry, universities and government."

9. A Strategic Industry at Risk

A Strategic Industry at Risk. A Report to the President and the Congress from the National Advisory Committee on Semiconductors. Chaired by Ian M. Ross, President, AT&T Bell Laboratories, November 1989.

This report describes the difficult competitive position faced by the semiconductor industry. "The semi-conductor industry, after an era of world leadership, is now in trouble ... It is imperative that the U.S. industry, in cooperation with government, develop a strategy to retain a strong semiconductor capability ... The loss of control of this large segment of the economy puts millions of jobs and billions of dollars in tax revenues in jeopardy."

10. Success Factors in Critical Technologies

Perspectives: Success Factors in Critical Technologies. Computer Systems Policy Project, Washington D.C., 1990.

A panel formed by 11 CEOs from the computer systems industry examines critical issues facing this industry. The main thrust of the report is the identification of 16 critical technologies, and 15 critical success factors. For each critical technology, the current and possible future U.S. competitive position is indicated as well as the role of the critical success factors.

11. Engineering Design

"The Neglect of Engineering Design," John Dixon and Michael Duffey, *California Management Review*, Vol. 32, 1990.

Among the research needs identified in this article is the development of the basis for a new generation of computer-aided mechanical design systems that integrate optimization and other mathematical tools with simulation of product and process operation. Industry-wide research and dissemination of the design-for-quality methodologies pioneered by Genichi Taguchi are called for.

Appendix B
Studies by the Mathematical Sciences Community

1. *Everybody Counts: A Report to the Nation on the Future of Mathematics Education.* Mathematical Sciences Education Board, Board on Mathematical Sciences, and Committee on the Mathematical Sciences in the Year 2000. National Academy Press, Washington D.C., 1989.

2. *A Challenge of Numbers: People in the Mathematical Sciences.* Mathematical Sciences Education Board, Board on Mathematical Sciences, and the Committee on the Mathematical Sciences in the Year 2000. National Academy Press, Washington, D.C., 1990.

3. *Renewing U.S. Mathematics: Critical Resource for the Future.* The Ad Hoc Committee on Resources for the Mathematical Sciences. National Academy Press, Washington, D.C., 1984.

4. *Renewing U.S. Mathematics: A Plan for the 1990s.* Committee on the Mathematical Sciences: Plans and Future Directions, Board on Mathematical Sciences. National Academy Press, Washington, D.C., 1990.

5. *Computational Modeling and Mathematics Applied to the Physical Sciences.* Committee on Applications of Mathematics. Office of Mathematical Sciences. National Academy Press, Washington, D.C., 1984.

6. *Future Directions in Computational Mathematics, Algorithms, & Scientific Software.* W. Rheinboldt, chair. Society for Industrial and Applied Mathematics, Philadelphia, 1985.

7. *Report of the Panel on Future Directions in Control Theory: A Mathematical Perspective.* W. Fleming, chair. Society for Industrial and Applied Mathematics, Philadelphia, 1990.

8. *Future Directions in Symbolic Computing.* A. Boyle and B. F. Caviness, eds. Society for Industrial and Applied Mathematics, Philadelphia, 1990.

9. *Cross-Disciplinary Research in the Statistical Sciences.* I. Olkin and J. Sacks, cochairs. Institute of Mathematical Statistics, Hayward, California, 1988.

10. *Nonlinear Optics.* Board on Mathematical Sciences, National Academy Press, Washington, D.C. 1991, in preparation.

11. *Selected Opportunities for Mathematical Sciences Research Related to the Navy Mission—An Update.* Panel on Applied Mathematics Research Alternatives for the Navy, Board on Mathematical Sciences. National Academy Press, Washington, D.C., 1990.

12. *Moving Beyond Myths: Revitalizing Undergraduate Mathematics.* Committee on the Mathematical Sciences in the Year 2000. Board on Mathematical Sciences. Mathematical Sciences Education Board. National Academy Press, Washington, D.C., 1991.